FOUNDERS IN FOCUS

FOUNDERS IN FOCUS

Stories from 14 Entrepreneurs Who Built It Their Way

By TJ Avazona
with Amy Goodson, Hillary Seiler, Dr. David Kenneth Waldman, Nick Day, Kenya Lee, Ryan Crittenden, Shailesh Poddar, Jessica Coffield, Michael Holt, Henry Criss, Dr. Adebola Ajao, Philip Shalala, Rich Funk, Christian Cassarly

THIN LEAF PRESS

In-Publication Data

Names: Avazona, TJ, Author, et al

Title: *Founders in Focus:* Stories from 14 Entrepreneurs Who Built It Their Way

ISBN 978-1-953183-88-0 (paperback) | 978-1-953183-89-7 (hardcover)

ISBN 978-1-953183-87-3 (ebook)

Business & Economics, Professional Development

Thin Leaf Press

TABLE OF CONTENTS

INTRODUCTION

By TJ Avazona

If you're browsing through this book, I can promise you're seeking something—perhaps it's a dream, a breakthrough, or a tiny glimmer of hope that you can create something your way. I'm TJ. Avazona, the man who brought all this together, and I've been where you are: bumbling around, crashing on my face more times than I care to count until I discovered one plain fact: you don't have to do it alone. Success is accelerated when you learn from others who've already trod the way. That is what *Founders in Focus* is all about.

I didn't come from a family of business entrepreneurs who were supportive of me. No high-brow dinners with conversation about startups or profits. I came from hardworking, good-ole everyday people who never had a clue about being a business owner. But me? I jumped in anyway, first, as a niche blogger back in 2017. Imagine me, bent over a wobbly laptop, clacking away at posts for 18 months full of late nights, half-baked concepts, and nobody reading. It was a complete flop. No fans, no cash—just a dented ego. So, I turned to YouTube automation in 2018, way before it was cool. I believed that faceless videos would set me up for riches. Nope. With next to zero views and no money, I was back to square one.

Then I tried my luck with a jewelry shop. I had bagged up hundreds of glittering trinkets like necklaces, earrings, and shiny stuff, hoping this would be the thing that stuck. Sales came in like a slow drip, enough to keep the lights on, but that's about it. Then came my foray into apparel—another huge miss. Failure after failure, I was overwhelmed by mountains of unsold merchandise, questioning what

I was doing incorrectly. I was doing my best but had no idea where I was falling short.

Everything changed when I stopped guessing. I found a mentor: someone who had already solved the puzzle I was unable to solve. He didn't simply throw me answers; he taught me an entirely new way to play the game. With him, I introduced a clothing product that took off, scaling it to $30K a month in an instant. I bought out another store and reached $45K a month. Money began flowing in, worry began dissipating, and I realized I had been attempting to reinvent the wheel when I should have simply questioned someone who had constructed one.

That's why I brought together 14 amazing entrepreneurs from diverse backgrounds, such as healthcare, real estate, coaching, tech, and more. I asked them deep questions, exploring their rough struggles, huge victories, and tricks that worked when everything else failed. Consider Hillary Seiler—she took a stack of medical bills from her mom's battle with an auto immune disease and developed Financial Footwork, enabling NFL rookies to build millions. Michael Holt joined forces with relatives to sell a £30 million London mansion as if there was no tomorrow. Dr. Adebola Ajao escaped FDA burnout to inspire women worldwide. Philip Shalala sniffed out $100 million ideas that no one else could see. These are not ideal fairy tales. These are actual, gritty, and full of teachings.

I have been the guy who was convinced I could do it all on my own. Spoiler alert: you don't have to. Every chapter is filled with key lessons I've extracted: plain, sturdy stuff you can apply, such as the good fortune Rich Funk found at a farmer's market or Amy Goodson's nutrition hustle. Something in here is going to click with you. You don't need a wealthy upbringing or a giant brain, just an openness to listen. These 14 wrote about their experiences so you can avoid some of the missteps I made. Choose a journey, take a tip, and build your thing your own way. Let's get going. Failing is part of it, but failing alone? That's just extra work we can avoid.

LEARNING THE HARD WAY SO YOU DON'T HAVE TO

By TJ Avazona

Picture teenage me, perched on a dirty curb at night, cars rushing by, headlights flashing as if they're laughing at me. I'm looking at my broken Nokia phone, its screen cracked and buttons sticky, when my friend comes running up, all worked up. "Pay-per-click, dude! You click things on the computer. They pay you a penny every time!" I'm thinking, hold up, what? But then my mind goes bright like a Christmas tree. Five hundred clicks a day—that's $5. In a month, $150! Get ten friends to click, too, and bam: $1500. I would be the richest kid on the block, no question. No computer at home, no laptop in sight. Just my rickety phone, chugging along on the slowest internet ever.

I began tapping away, solving those goofy captchas. Dog or toaster?

...and fantasizing about stacks of money.

But here's the kicker: it was all a scam. The actual cash was in Google AdSense, compensating people for blog traffic, but my penny-clicking job? Complete fake-out. I'd been conned, running after coins that didn't even exist. Nevertheless, that small thrill of "what if I could get big?" lingered with me. I didn't realize it yet, but I was already addicted to discovering a way to win.

That flop along the side of the road did not send me packing; I woke up. I was captivated by the prospect of amassing wealth on the internet, watching every video, podcast, and blog available to me, searching for the express lane to financial success. Initial attempt: health tips blog. Imagine me going through library books, writing things like "Eat Spinach and Feel Awesome," thinking others would read it, and profiting from affiliate links. I hustled, late nights, sleep-deprived eyes, and at last reached 100K visits. Big deal, right? Nope. The money? A couple of bucks a month. I had big dreams, but my wallet was still bare. Then I attempted niche blogs, such as Martin Luther King Day and Valentine's Day content, as well as small holiday ideas. Pros were earning $10K in a day with 100K live views on their sites.

I attempted to trail behind stars in my eyes, but it didn't work; not a single page ranked high enough to earn actual money. Total loss.

Then YouTube. Blogging was too competitive, I decided, "Videos are the way" I produced one, around dirt bike races for kids, and it rocketed up the charts, earning me $300. I'm jumping for joy, thinking I've hit the jackpot. But then, zilch. No other video made the cut. I began 12 channels, documentaries, 2D animations, giving them my heart and soul. YouTube closed them down, one by one. Accounts deleted, dreams shattered, back to square one.

Then I experimented with Fiverr. I learned graphic design, creating brochures, Facebook ads, and attractive covers, and began selling them for $10 each. People ordered, gradually but surely, and I thought, "This is something". Customers purchasing ads intrigued me; they were spending good money. Perhaps e-commerce was legit? I earned some money, but it wasn't life-altering.

I passed my account to a friend, "Keep it, I'm starting fresh." Another failure. E-commerce was my next grand attempt. Learned Shopify myself, sourced suppliers, learned advertising, the works. Released a radiant neck pendant, so lovely, I thought, "This is my millionaire maker" Scarcely 10 sales. No problem, I said, released over 25 other products, including hoodies, gadgets, and a plethora of different items. A year and a half gone and still nothing spectacular.

I'd sit up late, staring at unsold piles, crying in a corner, wondering why it wouldn't work. Saw a guy online bragging about $500K in hoodie sales.

I partnered with a Chinese vendor, experimented with some designs; it was okay, but not great. I was poor, exhausted, and at a loss.

The Mentor Miracle

Then one day, browsing Facebook, I struck gold. That hoodie guy was offering a course, actual lessons, not some hyped-up fake. I invested half my stash to enroll, I was literally his second student, viewing his vids like my life depended on it. He explained everything from finding products and setting up accounts to running ads and improving conversion rate. I religiously followed and my shop began buzzing, $5K a month, then $10K, reaching $130K in sales pronto I was going to be a millionaire, feeling invincible. But then, bam, Facebook suspended my ad account after I had invested some $50K. They had just provided me with a sexy manager, but a week later, zoom. Gone. I tried everything, new accounts, my cousins' accounts, and my friends' accounts, but all got shut down. It hurt bad.

However, I did have one wildcard, my deceased mother's active Facebook account. One evening, while having dinner and scrolling, I spotted it, a product yelling, "This is the one" My intuition was screaming at me to do it. I put in 40 hours of consecutive no-sleep work, created a store, spent ad money, and had everything set up. Month one: $1200. Month two: $5K. Month three: $12K. Month four: $25K. Month five: $45K to $47K. Sixth month, new store, heading towards $100K. I was on cloud nine until COVID came along and ruined everything. My shipment was held at a US port for three months. Refunds accumulated, $15 refund charges per one, thousands of dollars in ad money spent wasted, bad reviews everywhere.

It wasn't my fault, but my business was toast.

The Agency Takeoff

With my shipment held up, I slammed on the brakes. But I still knew ads like the back of my hand, so I began assisting others. Joined a Singapore-based agency that required realtors to conduct Zoom consultations during the COVID-19 pandemic. I went ahead and rolled out the campaigns, spending $10K, and one coach earned $100K, while another earned $120K. Paying $81 for a lead, I reduced it to $15, and they saved $200K. Helped another agency bring a horse saddle brand from $10K to $45K a month, and added $250K all in. Transformed a failed product in the Philippines into a ₱1.65M success within three months, yielding a 3.87 return.

That's when Avazona Ltd was born, my million-dollar PR and marketing agency. Now I'm the CEO, having worked with over 1,000 clients, big tech names like inGen Dynamics (worth $225M), Winden Bank, myChway, Good Calculator with 50M+ users, as well as celebrities like Tyga with 44M followers, and extraordinary brands like Margaritaville at Sea. From a roadside kid to rubbing elbows with stars, I had made it big.

My Big Wake-Up

My wake-up call was that hoodie dude sharing his entire game, opening stores, advertising, scaling it, all on camera. I cloned him, won big, and repeated it multiple times for clients. Here's what I learned: don't quit, two failed blogs, 12+ failed YouTube channels, 25+ product failures, a $100K store sunk, and a mature $ 50K+ spent ads account suspended. I persisted, and I'm here. Fail fast, the sooner you screw up, the sooner you figure out what doesn't work. Begin early, screw-ups as a teenager don't hurt as much. Continue learning; I learned design, ads, and Shopify all on my own, online, and for free. It's like adding tools to your toolbox.

Purpose of This Book: Your Turn to Shine

I've failed miserably, gotten back up, and discovered treasure because someone pointed me in the right direction. That's why I created this book, featuring 14 incredible individuals and their remarkable stories. I've been you, lost, doing everything, getting nowhere. These individuals, Hillary, Michael, Philip, screwed up too, then got it right. Their tales are your hacks. I came from running after pennies on a highway to having a million-dollar agency because I listened. Now it's your turn. Read these stories, take what feels right, and create something awesome. We're in this together, let's make it happen.

Key Takeaways

- *Mistakes Are Teachers:* I've had my share of flops: two blogs that went nowhere, 12 YouTube channels shut down, 25+ products that didn't sell a dime. Each one felt like a punch in the gut, but they weren't just losses. They were like little teachers showing me what to skip next time. That health blog with 100K visits but no cash? It taught me that traffic is good, but you need a strategy to make money. Those YouTube channels? Taught me not to spread myself too thin. Each stumble led me closer to what really works.
- *Helpers Save Time:* That hoodie guy's course was my saving grace; he taught me how to test small and scale big, and now I'm generating $100K in sales. If it weren't for him, I'd still be making guesses, losing years on things that didn't work. Mentors like him are a goldmine; now they've fallen over the stones already and can direct you to the straightaway. I transitioned from zero to major success quickly because I listened to someone who'd walked that road before. You don't have to map it out for yourself, borrow their map.
- *Mess Up Early:* Getting an early start spared me; those blog busts and roadside penny hunts during my teen years didn't

destroy me. If I had waited until I was older, with bills and responsibilities, those failures would have stung a whole lot worse. Messing up early, like my 25+ e-commerce flops, left me space to learn without the world coming crashing down. By the time I was prepared for actual victories, I had accumulated a heap of "what not to do." Start young, trip early, and you'll be tougher for it.

- *Learn Tons:* I couldn't afford classes, so I learned it all for free online—graphic design for Fiverr, Shopify for stores, and ads for clients. Each skill was like an extra tool in my box, and they built up to make me unstoppable. Creating ads introduced me to e-commerce, and buying ads helped grow my agency; none of that would have happened without learning. The internet is full of free lessons; grab them, experiment with them, and you'll be prepared for anything.
- *Trust Your Instincts:* That $45K-to-$100K product? I saw it during dinner time, and my gut yelled, "This is it." I pulled an all-nighter 40 hours straight to get it launched, and it took off, $1200, then $5K, all the way up to a $100K trajectory. Sure, I worked my butt off, but that initial spark was from within. When my head and heart were in agreement, I knew it was worth fighting for. Listen to that inner voice; it's smarter than you give it credit for.

THE PLAYBOOK FOR SUCCESS: TURNING GAPS INTO GAME-CHANGING OPPORTUNITIES

By Amy Goodson

Say hello to Amy Goodson, a whirlwind who spun her love for words, sports, and food into a game-changing career. With a degree in speech communications and no clear plan, she stumbled into sports nutrition by taking extra classes, working an unpaid internship, and simply persevering in an industry she knew little about. Today, as a registered dietitian and certified sports dietitian, Amy is the mastermind behind *The Sports Nutrition Playbook*, empowering athletes from high school fields to professional locker rooms. With 20 years of experience under her belt, including consulting for the Dallas Cowboys and over 1,600 media appearances, she has created her journey by saying "yes" to every opportunity and building solutions from the ground up. In this chapter, she answers questions that explain how passion, persistence, and flexibility turned uncertainty into influence, demonstrating that you don't need a straight line to make it happen; just the courage to keep moving and the ability to fill in gaps that others miss.

Amy, your career has been an incredible fusion of your passions for communication, sports, and nutrition. Could you take us back to the moment you realized you wanted to become a sports dietitian? What led you to this path?

My journey into sports nutrition wasn't strictly linear. My bachelor's degree was actually in speech communications because I had no clue what I wanted to do... I just knew I loved presenting and being in front of an audience. However, I also had a deep passion for exercise and nutrition, which led me to take a few nutrition courses, become a group fitness instructor, and minor in exercise physiology. That's when I came across the graduate program in exercise and sports nutrition at Texas Woman's University, and it all clicked into place.

It was tough becoming a registered dietitian, as it took three additional years of undergraduate and graduate coursework, which included some pretty intense sciences such as organic chemistry and biochemistry, and completing a full-time, unpaid 1,000-hour internship and passing the Registered Dietitian (RD) exam, but I never questioned whether it was the right path. I utilized every opportunity and went the extra mile in everything I did, which allowed me to work with all types of athletes, from high school to professional teams. Those early sacrifices built the foundation for my career, proving that when passion meets perseverance, doors open.

You transitioned from working in traditional sports nutrition roles to building multiple businesses under your own brand. What was the turning point that made you shift from a solopreneur to a full-scale entrepreneur?

For over a decade, I had my dream job, working with athletes from beginners to pros, but something inside me felt that "good" wasn't good enough. I was drawn to the gaps I saw in the sports nutrition industry; athletes needed practical, easy-to-access nutrition education, and dietitians needed clearer pathways to career success. I wanted to create solutions.

The big turning point came in 2020 when the world stood still. Pausing my speaking and media work provided a perfect window of opportunity to write *The Sports Nutrition Playbook*, something I had envisioned since 2013 but never had the time to complete. Once I self-published it, the demand was immediate. That momentum sparked the expansion of my brand, from individual coaching to hiring contract dietitians, launching an online mastermind course for registered dietitians who wanted to become sports dietitians, and starting *The Sports Nutrition Playbook Podcast*. What initially started as a solo mission became a business model catering to both athletes and dietitians.

Growing a business in the competitive health and sports industry is no easy feat. What were some of the biggest challenges you faced, and how did you overcome them?

One of the greatest challenges has been breaking into the professional sports industry. I was the first dietitian in all my roles, building programs from the ground up while earning trust from coaches, athletes, and support staff. The pressure was immense because, with elite sports, there isn't room for error. Excellence isn't optional; it's expected.

Another major challenge was scaling my business while maintaining quality. When you go from solopreneur to entrepreneur, you realize you can't do everything alone. At first, I handled everything from writing books to filling orders, consulting, coaching, and managing media. Eventually, I had to delegate, hire contract sports dietitians, and build structured service lines. That shift allowed me to focus on innovation rather than being stuck in the daily grind.

My solution to every challenge? Say "yes" to opportunities, build relationships, and stay relentlessly consistent. The key to breaking barriers is to show up, provide value, and always be prepared when an opportunity knocks.

Many entrepreneurs struggle with visibility and credibility. You've managed to build a powerful media presence with over 1,600 placements. What strategies helped you become a trusted voice in the industry?

The biggest game-changer was building upon my background in communication. I knew how to present complex nutrition concepts in a way that resonated with athletes, parents, coaches, and the media. That skill opened doors for me in speaking engagements, brand partnerships, and media/TV appearances.

My approach was threefold: First, I built relationships with journalists and producers, making myself an easy, reliable expert to call when they needed nutrition insight. Second, I was highly consistent; I didn't just wait for media opportunities, I created them by pitching relevant, timely topics. And third, I adapted to digital platforms early. As social media and online publications grew, I strategically positioned myself in spaces where my expertise was needed.

Most importantly, I never compromised on credibility. Science-backed, practical advice always came first. That commitment to quality ensured that once I gained visibility, I maintained trust, something that's crucial in health and nutrition.

Your work has been widely recognized, from industry awards to collaborations with major sports organizations. In your opinion, what sets your approach apart?

I believe my commitment to practical, actionable education truly differentiates my approach. While many nutrition professionals focus solely on theoretical knowledge, I emphasize application. Athletes, dietitians, and coaches don't just need information. They need clear, step-by-step strategies to integrate into their daily routines. This is why my content, whether in The Sports Nutrition Playbook, courses, or high school programs, is designed to be user-friendly and results-driven.

Another unique aspect of my work is my dual focus on professional development and consumer education. I believe the best way to expand sports nutrition is by empowering both professionals and athletes. By training registered dietitians through Amy Goodson RD Courses, I am creating a ripple effect by helping them launch careers that, in turn, provide athletes with the guidance they need.

Ultimately, my success comes from identifying unmet needs, creating solutions that are accessible and sustainable, and maintaining a reputation as a trusted expert in the field.

How do your mastermind and on-demand courses support registered dietitians and performance professionals in developing cultural competence and integrating social responsibility into their practice?

My mastermind and on-demand courses are designed to equip registered dietitians and performance professionals with the skills to integrate cultural competence and social responsibility into their practice. Through Amy Goodson RD Courses, I teach targeted education in this context to promote navigability through the sports nutrition complexities across different populations.

Cultural competence must exist in sports nutrition, as athletes come from different backgrounds with different dietary habits, traditions, and accessibility to resources. My courses deal with these differences, teaching professionals how to develop inclusive, adaptable nutrition plans that are sensitive to cultural preferences yet optimize their performance.

Furthermore, social responsibility is at the foundation of my work. Through initiatives such as the Sports Nutrition Game Plan, I am able to offer free resources to high school athletes, parents, and coaches, ensuring that sports nutrition education is levelly accessible to all, regardless of socioeconomic status. In mentoring dietitians and performance professionals, I enable them to act as champions for their athletes and communities and to create a more inclusive sports nutrition industry.

How does *The Sports Nutrition Playbook* empower high school athletes and small college sports programs to enhance athlete health and performance through its coaching, resources, and educational offerings? What other sources can the public turn to for further guidance?

The Sports Nutrition Playbook empowers high school athletes and small college sports programs with comprehensive education, tools, and resources to enhance athlete health and performance. It equips athletes, coaches, and athletic trainers with science-backed strategies to optimize fueling, hydration, and recovery through one-on-one performance nutrition coaching, consulting, and educational materials. The *Sports Nutrition Playbook Podcast* and YouTube channel offer free, accessible education to further support sports teams and families.

A unique initiative within my business is the *Sports Nutrition Game Plan*, a free high school nutrition program developed in partnership with the Texas Beef Council. This plug-and-play resource allows coaches and athletic staff to easily implement sports nutrition education within their teams, ensuring young athletes develop sustainable, performance-enhancing habits.

For those seeking additional guidance, professionals can explore *Amy Goodson RD Courses*, which offers specialized training for registered dietitians and performance professionals. The Sports Nutrition Playbook is revolutionizing how high school and small college athletes fuel their performance and long-term health through increased access to expert-driven sports nutrition.

Your mission is to "Serve as a credible and reliable source of food and nutrition information to educate the everyday consumer and the public at large." What are some of your founding principles that you believe help you maintain relevance and stay ahead of the game?

One of my core strategies has been conducting nontraditional market research. I built my programs by paying attention to the questions I was asked repeatedly over and over again throughout my 20 years in the field. Instead of relying solely on surveys or trends, I created solutions that directly addressed the most common concerns of athletes, parents, coaches, and dietitians.

Another key strategy has been diversifying my services. While many dietitians focus solely on private practice, I expanded into media work, speaking engagements, book publishing, and digital courses. This allowed me to build a reputation as an industry leader while also creating multiple revenue streams.

Finally, I have prioritized relationships and credibility. Being recognized as a media expert and working with organizations like the National Dairy Council and the American Heart Association has strengthened my brand's trustworthiness. My advice to aspiring professionals is to establish authority in their niche and continuously adapt to industry needs.

How do you personally define health, and how does that definition influence the work you do in the nutrition and wellness space?

Health, to me, is a holistic balance of proper nutrition, physical activity, and overall well-being. It's not just about what you eat but about how you fuel your body to perform at its best, whether you're an elite athlete or someone striving for daily wellness. This belief is at the core of my work in sports nutrition and wellness education.

Through Amy Goodson RD Courses and The Sports Nutrition Playbook, I empower athletes, parents, coaches, and performance professionals with evidence-based strategies to optimize performance and long-term health.

Recognizing the gap in sports nutrition services, especially at the high school and smaller college levels, I created accessible programs that bridge education and practical implementation. My Sports Nutrition Game Plan program provides free, structured guidance to underserved high school athletes and schools, while my RD Internship offers dietitians hands-on experience to expand career opportunities in this growing field by working with those athletes and programs. By combining professional education with real-world application, I aim to elevate both individual health outcomes and industry standards. My mission is to ensure that athletes at every level have access to quality nutrition guidance, helping them achieve peak performance while producing a lifetime of wellness.

I know it's impossible to sum up your entire journey in one answer, but if you had to start from scratch today, knowing everything you know now, how would you do it? In short, what's the single most valuable lesson you would share with others who want to be like you?

If I had to start over, I would focus on two things: networking strategically and building scalable systems from day one. Relationships have been the cornerstone of my success. Every significant career opportunity came from a recommendation, a connection, or someone vouching for my work. If you want to grow fast, you must put yourself in rooms with the right people and offer value before expecting anything in return.

The second lesson is to create systems that allow you to scale. In the beginning, I did everything manually, from coaching to shipping books. But real growth comes when you set up efficient processes, whether it's hiring the right people, leveraging technology, or automating tasks and processes through a CRM (Client Relationship Management system), which we now offer to other performance and wellness professionals through Amy Goodson RD Courses.

Above all, the most valuable lesson I've learned is that success isn't about luck but preparation and meeting opportunity. Be relentlessly consistent, keep showing up, and say "yes" until you can afford to say "no." That's how you turn passion into a thriving business.

Key Takeaways

- Take the Winding Path: Amy's path from speech to sports nutrition was not intentional; extra courses and a volunteer job led her down this path. She loved the detour, wrapping up with the Dallas Cowboys years later. Twists don't ruin you; they define your own path if you remain open to them.
- Take the Pause: The 2020 slowdown gave rise to *The Sports Nutrition Playbook*. Amy wrote while everyone else waited. Forced pause isn't a stall; it's an opportunity to construct what's been simmering, turning quiet into your loudest launch.
- Scale by Letting Go: Independent work has reached a plateau. She brought in help to focus on strategy, not tedium. Her company doubled in size when she delegated the nitty-gritty details to others. Growth means delegating smartly to dream bigger.
- Credibility Wins Trust: 1,600+ media spots didn't happen because of hype. Amy brought science-based value every time. Continuously arriving with real insight earned her airtime and credibility. Substance over flash opens doors that stick.
- Fill the Gaps: Free high school talks and dietitian mentoring emerged from recognizing needs that were being ignored, athletes being clueless about fuel, and professionals needing

guidance. She jumped in, and impact followed. Success hits when you solve what others skip.

- Say Yes to Grow: Saying "yes" to everything landed her initial gigs, which were challenging and hard-scrabble, establishing her credibility. Years down the line, she chooses her "no's." Early hustle is not forever; it's the launching pad for subsequent freedom.

THE POWER OF SELF-BELIEF: TURNING FINANCIAL STRUGGLES INTO A GAME PLAN FOR SUCCESS

By Hillary Seiler

Meet our next superstar, Hillary Seiler, whose money smarts grew from a kitchen table buried in bills during her family's seven-year health fight. As a leading mortgage lender and now educator, she recognized that wealthier people struggled with fundamental financial concepts, so she created a solution to address this problem. Financial Footwork offers a sports-themed approach to transform complex economic situations into a structured understanding through diligent determination. The former NFL rookie coach, Hillary Seiler, has achieved status as one of the Top 50 Financial Keynote Speakers in addition to her work mentoring NFL rookies. Using her survivor's instincts and determination, she overcame adversity because she did not have any silver spoon advantages. In this chapter, she answers questions that recount the story of how adversity drove her to launch her mission, demonstrating that through consistent decision-making and unwavering determination, one can transform one's financial narrative.

You've built a fascinating career as a financial educator, keynote speaker, and entrepreneur. Before we dive into your journey, can you take us back to the beginning? How did you first get interested in financial literacy, and how did that lead to the creation of Financial Footwork?

My journey into finance didn't begin in a classroom or a boardroom—it started at home during one of the hardest times my family ever faced. I was 19 when my mom got sick, and for the next seven years, we were locked in a financial and emotional battle, making high-stakes decisions every day.

I still remember sitting at the kitchen table as my dad laid everything out—bills, expenses, the full financial reality. No sugarcoating. Just truth and a promise to face it together. That conversation set the tone. We learned how to stretch every dollar, navigate medical debt, and make impossible choices—treatment or mortgage, groceries or gas.

Money stopped being numbers on a screen. It became stress, sacrifice, and survival. It controlled everything—treatment options, keeping the lights on, planning beyond the next crisis. The pressure was crushing. But what held us together was communication. My dad made sure we all understood where we stood. That transparency made us active participants—we weren't just along for the ride. We were solving problems and making decisions together.

Watching the strain unfold, I came to a hard truth: most people don't get a financial playbook. They're thrown in, forced to learn by trial and error, and the consequences can be brutal. I knew I wanted to change that. I wanted to give people the tools, knowledge, and confidence to take control before they hit a wall.

That experience shaped everything I do now. It's why I teach money the way I do—straightforward, practical, real. I coach people to train for financial fitness like an athlete trains for a game—through preparation, discipline, and strategy. Everyone deserves a plan they can actually use.

Before coaching, I worked as a top mortgage lender and finance professional. Those years were a training ground. I helped people through major decisions—buying homes, refinancing debt, planning for the future. But even with all the success, something was missing. I wasn't teaching people how to build long-term financial security on their own.

In lending, I saw how little financial literacy most people had, even when making life-changing decisions. Big moves—like taking out a mortgage—were often made without a clear understanding of how it all connected. I watched people take risks they didn't fully grasp, and I realized many were treating money as a one-time problem, not a lifelong process that demands strategy and consistency.

As a top mortgage lender on the West Coast, I closed countless deals, but it often felt like damage control—helping people through the moment without addressing the habits and planning that could prevent future crises. Over time, my focus shifted. I wanted to teach people how to build a strong financial foundation—not just get by.

That's when it clicked. I wasn't just here to help people through transactions. I was here to equip them for life. My work in finance taught me that true financial health comes from understanding how everything fits together—debt, savings, investing, and decision-making. That realization drove me to create Financial Footwork. I wanted a system that didn't just offer quick fixes but gave people a real, sustainable path forward—one they could carry through every stage of life.

Financial Footwork stands out because of its focus on professional athletes. What inspired you to combine financial literacy with sports principles like discipline and strategy? Were there any moments or stories that showed you that professional athletes required financial guidance to succeed better?

My journey in finance began in banking, but it didn't take long to notice a glaring gap—especially when it came to athletes. Having grown up around sports, I saw how even high-earning athletes often had no idea how to manage their money. They were making millions without a game plan. No one explained taxes, protecting earnings, or how to make their wealth last beyond their careers. It was a frustrating pattern, and I knew I had to step in.

Everything changed when I got a call from Athlete Transitions University. I was invited to interview for a financial coach position, but instead of a sit-down meeting, I walked into a five-day workshop with retiring athletes. Right away, I knew this was more than a job interview. These athletes didn't need someone to throw numbers at them—they needed a guide who understood their world and could help them navigate life after sports.

Over the week, I worked side by side with them on managing post-career finances and planning for the future. We covered taxes, investing, and budgeting—all through a lens they could relate to. I connected the habits that made them elite athletes—discipline, structure, focus—to building smart financial routines. As the workshop went on, they became more engaged, asking sharp questions and recognizing how much power came with financial knowledge. I could see it landing. They weren't just learning; they were owning it.

What I didn't know was that the workshop doubled as an audition for a role with the Miami Dolphins. By the end of the week, they'd seen enough. I was hired to help guide their rookies in building strong financial habits from day one. That single call became the launchpad for everything that followed. It proved that my approach—

practical, direct, and tailored to real life—could create an impact at the highest levels of sport.

That experience inspired me to launch Financial Footwork. I wanted a system that trained people to manage money with the same intensity they brought to sports. Money management isn't something you wing. It's a skill that requires repetition, discipline, and strategy. That's why I built My Money Playbook, a structured program that breaks down personal finance into clear, trainable steps.

I still remember those first workshops. I stood in front of young athletes who had just signed contracts bigger than they ever imagined. They were focused and driven but financially unprepared. We talked about taxes, spending, and investing. Some had already made costly mistakes. Others didn't know where to start. The need was clear—and urgent.

That was the turning point. These athletes needed financial education as much as they needed training schedules and game plans. They needed something built for their world—in their language, with a strategy they could follow. Because once the games stop, the money has to keep working. Without a plan, even the biggest contracts can disappear. That's what Financial Footwork delivers—a real, usable playbook for managing money and building a secure future.

Financial literacy faces significant barriers because people encounter wrong information combined with constrained accessibility to essential knowledge. Working with NFL and NBA teams and major universities and corporations has revealed to the financial myths athletes often believe. What is your method for dismantling such obstacles?

One of the biggest challenges in financial literacy is breaking through misinformation and making financial education accessible, especially for athletes who are often targeted with bad advice. Working with NFL and NBA teams, universities, and corporations, I've seen the same myths come up repeatedly—things like "I'll always make this much money," "Investing is only for the wealthy," or "I don't need to budget because I have a financial advisor." These misconceptions can lead to major financial missteps.

My approach to dismantling these barriers is rooted in three key principles: education, repetition, and application. First, I break down complex financial concepts into clear, actionable steps. I don't just tell athletes what they should do—I show them how money actually works in their world, using real-life scenarios and numbers that make sense for them.

Second, I use repetition, just like in sports training. No athlete masters their game after one practice, and the same goes for financial literacy. I build structured financial workouts that reinforce key money habits over time, so these principles become second nature.

Finally, I focus on application. Knowledge isn't enough—it's about execution. I help athletes apply what they learn immediately, whether it's reviewing contracts, setting up savings systems, or understanding taxes. The goal is to give them a financial playbook they can follow throughout their careers and beyond, ensuring they build long-term wealth and financial stability.

Athletes have access to financial advisors, yet many still struggle with money management. What strategies did you use, and when did you realize that your breakthrough work was making a gigantic impact?

Having a financial advisor is important, but their job is to build and protect wealth—not to manage an athlete's daily financial choices. No advisor can outwork bad spending habits, and no investment strategy can make up for reckless cash flow decisions. Wealth isn't gained or lost in one big move—it's built (or drained) in the day-to-day.

For many athletes, the real challenge isn't understanding money—it's managing emotions, environment, and habits. Emotional spending is a huge issue. With the pressure to look successful, support family, and enjoy the rewards of their hard work, it's easy to justify overspending. But financial stability doesn't come from making money—it comes from keeping it. Every dollar spent is a choice, and those choices add up fast.

Environment plays a huge role, too. I've seen athletes lose millions simply because they had the wrong people around them—bad business deals, excessive handouts, or financial "advisors" who didn't have their best interests at heart. One of the first things I teach is how to evaluate your financial circle. If the people around you encourage reckless spending instead of smart money moves, it's time to make a change.

That's why I focus so much on daily financial habits. While financial advisors handle investments, tax strategies, and long-term planning, it's up to the individual to manage what happens between paychecks. That means tracking cash flow, setting spending limits, and automating savings—just like an athlete follows a training schedule. I always tell players, "You don't get in shape by working out once; you train consistently. Your money works the same way."

I knew my work was making a real impact when athletes began texting me months or even years later, telling me they finally had savings for the first time, they could buy a home, invest in a business, set boundaries with family, or walk away from bad deals because they understood what was at stake. One of my players even texted me, *You saved my life. Now I know I can do this.* That was a huge moment for me. The biggest wins aren't just in the numbers—it's in the mindset shift that helps them build wealth for life. The advisors build the strategy, but the execution happens in everyday decisions. And that's exactly where I help them take control.

There are many financial educators, but very few successfully build an entire business around it. What were some of the biggest hurdles you faced while launching and scaling Financial Footwork? Were there any early mistakes that, looking back, became valuable lessons?

Starting a business is never easy, and mine was no exception. The challenges weren't just financial or logistical—they were about changing mindsets. One of my biggest hurdles was convincing organizations, both corporate and athletic, that financial literacy isn't just a "nice-to-have"—it's a necessity.

Early on, I faced resistance. Teams focused on performance. Companies focused on revenue. No one wanted to talk about money—at least, not in a way that addressed the financial struggles their employees and players were actually facing. I had to show them what they couldn't see: that financial stress kills performance. An athlete can't focus on the game if they're losing sleep over bad investments or unpaid taxes. An employee can't bring their best to work if they're drowning in debt and afraid to check their bank account. Financial literacy isn't just about wealth—it's also well-being, stability, and long-term success.

I knew I had to back up my passion with hard facts. I gathered data, case studies, and real-life examples of athletes and employees who had suffered because they lacked financial education. I showed teams how financial stress leads to poor decision-making, short careers, and lost potential. I showed companies how money problems drive turnover, burnout, and decreased productivity. Slowly, doors started opening, but getting in was just the first step.

The real challenge came when it was time to scale. As demand for my coaching grew, I had to figure out how to deliver real, high-impact financial education at scale—without losing the personal, hands-on approach that made Financial Footwork successful. That meant getting creative. I built out digital resources, on-demand training, and structured coaching programs that could be implemented across multiple organizations without sacrificing effectiveness. I developed My Money Playbook, a system that allows people to train their money like an athlete trains for their sport—step by step, with drills, strategies, and measurable progress.

Of course, the challenges weren't just professional. They were deeply personal, too. There were moments when I questioned if I was making a difference. Days when rejection hit like a brick wall. Nights when exhaustion crept in, making me wonder if all the effort was worth it. The pressure of breaking boundaries, proving myself in rooms where no one expected me to succeed, and constantly pushing forward—it was heavy.

But here's the thing: I knew exactly what was at stake. This wasn't just business for me. This was personal. This was my passion. Every time an athlete told me they felt in control of their financial future, or an employee shared that they finally understood their paycheck and felt empowered instead of anxious, or when I saw the lightbulb go on for someone who had been struggling for years, I knew I was exactly where I needed to be.

That's what keeps me going. Financial education isn't just about teaching people to save money—it's giving them freedom, power, and peace of mind.

You've been recognized as a Top 50 Financial Keynote Speaker and have built Financial Footwork into a trusted brand. If you had to pinpoint three foundational principles that have driven your business success, what would they be?

At the core of Financial Footwork is a belief that financial education changes lives. Whether I'm working with athletes, corporate teams, or individuals, I've seen how understanding money leads to better decisions, less stress, and stronger long-term outcomes. But teaching facts alone isn't enough. Financial learning has to be clear, engaging, and actionable. From day one, I set out to break away from the dry, jargon-heavy approach that turns people off. Whether through interactive workshops, one-on-one coaching, or tools like My Money Playbook, my goal has always been to spark interest—and more importantly, confidence. I want people to walk away knowing they can manage their finances without having to lean on someone else every time they hit a decision point. That kind of independence is powerful.

Finance can feel overwhelming, especially when it's buried under confusing terms and complex ideas. One of the guiding principles behind Financial Footwork has been to simplify. Instead of flooding people with information, I break things down into manageable steps that build momentum. I'm not interested in lecturing or adding pressure. I focus on helping people start where they are and make steady progress, one clear step at a time. Financial literacy should be accessible and even enjoyable. There's no reason money management has to feel out of reach—it just needs the right approach. Whether someone is just beginning or refining their strategy, they should feel like finance is something they can do.

What drives long-term results, though, isn't just knowledge—it's mindset. The habits we build daily, often in quiet moments, shape the outcomes we see later. From the beginning, I understood that emotional control, discipline, and consistent effort play as big a role as knowing how to budget or invest. That's why I coach with an eye on behavior, not just information. Athletes learn to manage their environments and emotions; individuals learn to stay disciplined through distractions and setbacks. Progress doesn't come from occasional big wins. It comes from small, repeated efforts, especially when things get hard. That's where change takes hold.

These ideas—accessible education, a simplified approach, and a focus on mindset—have been the foundation of Financial Footwork's growth. They continue to shape my work every day, guiding people to train their money with the same intensity they bring to every other part of their lives.

Your programs are used by corporations, athletes, and universities alike. How did you design Financial Footwork to be adaptable for such diverse audiences? Were there any particular challenges in creating a model that could work for both a corporate employee and an NFL player?

The great thing about financial literacy is that the fundamentals are universal. Whether you're an NFL player, a corporate employee, or a university student, the core financial concepts—budgeting, saving, investing—are the same for everyone. The real challenge is finding a way to make those concepts accessible and actionable for such diverse audiences. That's where the approach at Financial Footwork comes in.

I designed Financial Footwork to be adaptable by treating financial education like a fitness program. Think about how athletes train: they follow a structured plan with drills and habits that build over time. I took that same mentality and applied it to money. The idea is simple—just like any physical training program, you can train your money, one step at a time. You don't have to master everything at once. It's the small, consistent habits that add up to big change. This method works across different audiences because it taps into something that everyone can relate to: building habits over time.

For athletes, I focus on discipline, strategy, and managing emotions—things they already know how to do in their sport. The principles of financial success—being smart with your money, building a strong foundation, and investing in the future—aren't any different for them than they are for someone working in a corporate environment. For corporate employees, I help them understand how to apply those same principles to their career, personal life, and long-term goals.

The real breakthrough is that once people realize the connection between training their bodies and training their money, it clicks. They start to see the value of building habits that become second nature, whether it's sticking to a budget or developing a mindset that keeps them on track. I am to give people the tools and confidenceto manage their finances the way athletes manage their training—step by step, with a long-term view in mind.

So, yes, the challenge was making sure the model could be flexible enough to work for such a wide range of people. But by focusing on the foundational principles of finance and applying a fitness-like mentality, anyone can train their money and set themselves up for financial success, no matter where they're starting from.

On *The Burn Podcast*, you talked about the importance of mindset in financial success. What mental habits or beliefs do you see holding people back the most when it comes to money, and how do you help them shift into a healthier financial mindset?

Mindset is everything when it comes to financial success. I'm often quoted saying, "Money is 99% mindset and 1% math," because I truly believe that. I see so many people get stuck in mental habits or beliefs that hold them back, and they don't even realize it. One of the biggest ones I encounter is the idea that money is "bad" or that it's not meant for everyone to have a lot of it. People get hung up on these limiting beliefs—whether it's because of how they were raised, what they've seen, or just old misconceptions about wealth.

Another big one is fear—fear of making mistakes with money, fear of not having enough, or fear of looking bad in front of others. This fear keeps people paralyzed and prevents them from taking control of their finances. Then there's the "I'm not good with money" mindset. When people say that, it's like they've already written themselves off. That mindset becomes a self-fulfilling prophecy.

So, how do I help them shift? First, I meet people where they are. I don't tell them to "just think positive" or "change your beliefs overnight." It's more about focusing on small, consistent actions that build confidence and create positive momentum. We start with the basics—learning how to manage money on a practical level: budgeting, saving, and understanding credit. Once people begin to see that they *can* make smart decisions with their money, the fear starts to fade, and those limiting beliefs begin to crumble.

I also help them reframe their thinking around money as a tool to create freedom, stability, and opportunities. Money is just a resource, and when people start thinking of it that way, they're more likely to take ownership of it. I've seen this shift happen countless times—once people start seeing money as something they can control and use for their benefit, their entire mindset changes.

The key is consistent education and taking the pressure off. Financial wellness doesn't have to be overwhelming—it can be simple, manageable, and empowering. When people feel like they're in control, that's when they can truly shift into a healthier financial mindset and start making choices that set them up for long-term success.

As an entrepreneur, how has building Financial Footwork changed you personally? Have there been any defining moments that made you step back and think, Wow, I never imagined I'd be here?

Building Financial Footwork has changed me in ways I didn't expect. When I reached my 10th NFL team, I paused to take it in. That was a real moment—so was breaking into the NBA. But the biggest realizations haven't come from the headlines. They've come from the steady progress, the daily work that adds up over time. Those smaller wins have shaped me just as much as the big ones, and they're what keep me moving forward.

Each time I step into a new space—whether with a team, a company, or a university—I feel the momentum building. There have been plenty of moments when I felt frustrated or worn down, but the breakthroughs reminded me why this matters. It's not just about growth on paper. It's about watching change take hold in real-time.

The business growth has gone hand-in-hand with personal growth. This journey has pushed me to face things I might've once avoided and rise to challenges I wasn't sure I was ready for. The most rewarding part isn't the accolades—it's seeing how the work is landing, how it's helping people take control of their lives in ways they didn't think were possible. Along the way, I've formed lasting friendships and meaningful collaborations. These relationships have opened doors, deepened my reach, and strengthened the communities we work with.

When I look back at what's been built over the past decade, I'm still surprised sometimes by how far it's come. The path hasn't been smooth, but it's been worth every step. None of this would exist without the people around me. This has never been about going it alone. From the athletes who trusted me to the team that's been by my side, every success has been shared. Every win reflects a collective effort. That support is the foundation—and it's what keeps me showing up to do the work.

I know it's impossible to sum up your entire journey in one answer, but if you had to start from scratch today, knowing everything you know now, how would you do it? In short, what's the single most valuable lesson you would share with aspiring entrepreneurs?

If I had to start from scratch today, knowing everything I know now, the biggest lesson I would share is this: Believe in yourself, no matter what. It sounds simple, but it's the most powerful tool you can have as an entrepreneur. When I was starting out, there were plenty of people who didn't think this journey was even possible. They doubted me, laughed at the idea, or threw out sarcastic remarks like, "Good luck with that." But what kept me going was the unwavering belief from two people who had my back from day one—who truly believed, without hesitation, that I could make this happen.

I won't lie, there were moments when I had my doubts. I still remember those days when the weight of negativity, from both external sources and my own fears, would creep in. But I knew deep down that my conviction and my passion for helping people were stronger than those doubts. I chose to leave the haters in the past and keep pushing forward because the impact I knew I could make in people's lives kept me going. My vision was clear, and the desire to see it come to life outweighed the thoughts that told me it couldn't happen.

But you have to have self-belief and an unwavering passion for what you're doing. Without those two, you won't make it to the finish line. Entrepreneurship is a long, winding road. It's one I was more than willing to brave because I knew how powerful my vision was, and I was determined to see it through. Entrepreneurship isn't a straight path. You probably won't hit your actual destination, but the pursuit of it is worth every step. The journey, the challenges, and the constant evolution of your vision are how you grow as an entrepreneur.

So my advice? Block out the negativity. People will always have opinions, but your vision is yours, and if you're determined enough, you can make it happen. When you're your own biggest believer, that energy is unstoppable. Trust your journey, stay focused, and know that your belief in yourself is the foundation that will carry you through any challenge.

Key Takeaways

- Struggle Shapes Purpose: Seven years' worth of medical expenses did not defeat Hillary; they ignited her fire. Financial Footwork developed from that destruction and helped others avoid her pain. Hardship isn't only a test; it's a teacher if you harness it.
- Spot the Gap, Fill It: NFL rookies who cashed fat checks but didn't know what to do with them guided her playbook. She constructed what they didn't have: easy, practical money know-how. Identifying others' shortcuts is where value and victory begin.

- Mindset Beats Math: "99% mindset, 1% math" is not a slogan, it's her reality. Teaching a pro athlete to save changed his mindset, not just his bank account. Belief and habits win over number-crunching, hands down.
- Train Money Like a Muscle: Sports drills become money drills, with daily reps of budgeting and saving. Clients stuck with it, cutting debt in months. Consistency, not genius, builds financial strength that lasts.
- Prove It to Win It: Teams balked at her ideas, but she presented data showing that rookies saved 20% more. Results silenced doubters, opening the doors to the NFL. Evidence turns "no" into "yes" when you've got the goods.
- Trust When Nobody Else Will: Lenders laughed, but Hillary continued to pitch. Self-belief took her to keynote stages. Doubt is loud. You believe your vision must be more audible to cut through.

MARSHALING HARMONY AND MUSIC THROUGH EMPATHETIC LEADERSHIP

By Dr. David Kenneth Waldman

From a 1.2 GPA to a Ph.D., meet Dr. David Kenneth Waldman, whose shattered pre-med dream, thwarted by math woes, unlocked a 40-year mission in education and gender justice. Since establishing To Love Children Educational Foundation International in 2002, he has used the organization to provide vulnerable girls from Thailand with education that leads to success in the United Nations halls. Waldman filled his career trajectory with a Ph.D. in Public Policy, combined with children's publications and a romance novel that won the prestigious Weep for Love Award. Living with depression instilled a deep compassion in him, and his musical skills enabled him to lead diverse teams worldwide. The UN Consultative Status, along with his honors, has helped David to align grassroots dedication with his policy influence. Throughout this section, the author explains how determination, coupled with optimism, transformed challenges into transformative change, demonstrating that a single voice developed through hardship can distinctively help countless individuals.

Dr. Waldman, you have more than 40 years of experience in education, social entrepreneurship, and public policy. Can you take us back to the beginning? What drove your lifelong passion for education, and how has your vision changed over the decades?

College began with a detour that reshaped my personal and professional path. My journey has never followed a straight line. Each career step—from textbook consultant to children's author to advocating for girls' education in Uganda—has been part of a broader mission rooted in education and service.

As a child, I dreamed of becoming a doctor. I was eager, sitting on a lab stool in my first pre-med biology course. Then came the moment that changed everything—an academic official pulled me from class to inform me I lacked the math prerequisites. That news ended my pre-med path before it began. With no Plan B, I wandered academically, taking courses without direction.

During sophomore year, I had to declare a major. Intuition led me to education, one of the few programs without a math requirement. I excelled in my coursework and graduated in 1976 with a degree in Elementary Education, the first step in a lifelong journey shaped by resilience and the belief that opportunity always returns.

This degree opened many doors. I began creating educational programs for vulnerable girls using a multidisciplinary approach. I adopted the principle, "What I say, I do," as a leadership tenet. I believe leaders should model the change they want to see.

My path led to writing children's books and hosting a radio show on the Blind Radio Network, where I explored children's literature and creative approaches to education. Depression visited me in waves over the years, deepening my empathy for at-risk children. While not every child could be saved, I found new purpose by inspiring global volunteers—focusing on one child at a time.

In 1993, while visiting Northern Thailand near the Laos border, I sponsored a three-year-old girl and had an epiphany that changed my life. I later founded the To Love Children Educational Foundation International Inc., dedicated to educating vulnerable girls. This work taught me that real change happens at the local level, in partnership with community leaders.

Earning a Master's in International Relations and later a Ph.D. in Public Policy and Public Administration helped bridge theory with practice. These academic milestones deepened my understanding of gender justice, human rights, and cultural complexity—strengthening my mission to create sustainable educational opportunities for girls worldwide.

Your organization, To Love Children Educational Foundation International Inc., has had a remarkable impact on gender justice and sustainable girls' education. What was the turning point or experience that compelled you to create this organization?

Recognizing the importance of education for vulnerable girls shaped how I approached leadership, writing, and social entrepreneurship. For over five decades, education has been the common thread connecting my roles as author, publisher, and founder of a nonprofit organization.

"Don't just say you have read books. Show that through them you have learned to think better, to be a more discriminating and reflective person. Books are the training weights of the mind. They are very helpful, but it would be a bad mistake to suppose that one has made progress simply by having internalized their contents." – Epictetus. This quote reminded me that reading alone isn't enough—action must follow insight.

In 1993, my path shifted. I sponsored a three-year-old girl living in a small village near the Laos border in Northern Thailand. On my first visit, I walked down a dirt road past a black water buffalo. The moment was ordinary, but something in it struck me. I experienced an epiphany—a sudden clarity that this child, and others like her, were part of my purpose.

I didn't yet know how to begin, only that I needed to act. Over time, a clearer understanding took shape. In 2002, I founded the To Love Children Educational Foundation International, a nonprofit committed to creating educational opportunities for vulnerable children, especially girls, in developing countries.

I've learned to follow the signs that align with my values. Missed chances often stem not from failure but from hesitation or inaction. Each step forward came through persistence, not certainty. Progress wasn't always linear, but determination kept me moving.

Over 25 years, I've worked to build educational programs that lead to lasting social change. When the foundation was granted Special Consultative Status with the UN's Economic and Social Council in 2006, it opened a new chapter—one of advocacy and collaboration at the global level.

In this work, I've learned from policymakers, educators, and community leaders. I've leaned into an empathetic leadership style that values harmony and the kind of influence that builds, rather than commands. These experiences have deepened my belief that change begins with opportunity, and opportunity begins with education.

You've managed to bring together grassroots communities and senior government policymakers to shape educational policy. What were some of the challenges you encountered in bridging this divide? How challenging was working with both local communities and global policymakers?

The global development space is crowded, with countless NGOs competing for limited resources and attention. The real challenge lies in focusing on rural communities in Uganda, where sustainable educational opportunities for girls are most needed.

Wherever I traveled, I was met with warmth and openness from people who recognized the sincerity of our mission.

Gaining Consultative Status with the United Nations gave our organization a platform to contribute at the global level. It allowed us to present policy recommendations and engage in discussions that influence international agendas. But real change happens locally. Building strong ties with community leaders helped bypass political roadblocks and focus on creating practical solutions rooted in trust and collaboration.

People from different cultures and backgrounds consistently responded to our efforts with respect and encouragement. What stalled our progress wasn't the work itself—it was funding. Fundraising remained the central obstacle to growing the nonprofit's reach and sustaining long-term programs.

Through research in gender justice and human rights, I began to understand the deeper systemic challenges facing girls in poverty. A recurring pattern emerged: girls were not only excluded by economic hardship but also by a lack of legal protections and gender justice frameworks. The United States, for instance, remains one of the few countries that hasn't ratified the Convention on the Rights of the Child—a clear indication of its limited leadership in this space.

Despite financial constraints, our impact grew by relying on committed volunteers. Those who aligned with our mission became essential partners. We created an environment where ideas were shared, problems were solved collectively, and responsibility was distributed. When volunteers felt ownership, their investment deepened. This collaborative approach became our greatest strength.

The result was a growing network that bridged grassroots efforts with senior policymakers. We were invited to the table with government leaders, UN agencies like UNICEF, and royalty—including a meeting with the King of the Busoga Kingdom in Uganda. One of the highlights was an invitation to speak at the first Science for Girls conference held at the United Nations in New York.

You've received Special Consultative Status with the United Nations Economic and Social Council. What does this mean for your work, and how has it allowed you to make genuine change on an international scale?

Obtaining Special Consultative Status with the Economic and Social Council United Nations 2006 permitted access to a plethora of resources such as expertise, human rights scholars, and world leaders who affect social change. I've had multiple chances to submit policy papers to the U.N. record, which may hopefully influence governmental officials at all levels at the U.N. The intended outcome is to open doors to reach a broader global audience. How do you quantitatively measure social, educational, and economic change on a local scale? Numbers mute any meaning to a reality of small individual change that may take years to realize its effect.

As a gender justice expert, you've spent considerable time working on policies concerning girls' education. What are the most prominent barriers still impeding progress, and how do you think they can be addressed?

Social change requires a multidisciplinary approach involving collaboration across various sectors. Efforts span from improving school access for girls and providing food programs to ensuring year-round education through menstrual hygiene support. Equally urgent is building coalitions to combat child sex trafficking. While curriculum resources and internet access are vital, they pale in comparison to the crisis of girls being trafficked into sexual slavery. Effective solutions demand immediate action, yet implementation is hindered by fragmented agendas and a lack of cohesion between governments and nonprofit organizations. This division undercuts any unified approach to prevention and mental health support for survivors reentering their communities.

My doctoral thesis explored how human rights and cultural practices shape gender justice outcomes for girls. This wasn't framed as a competition between human rights and gender justice but as a call to align theory with practice through long-term commitment. The central argument was that gender justice remains a missing element in advancing girls' education in many regions.

Despite ongoing United Nations mandates promoting gender equality, achieving local justice for girls has remained difficult. Grounded in theories from Sally Engle Merry on cultural particularism and Amartya Sen on comparative justice, and supported by Adele Clarke's situational analysis framework, the research examined how local customs and beliefs obstruct gender equity.

The study investigated the roles and perspectives of those working on gender, cultural, and human rights issues across international and national settings. Using a qualitative approach, I conducted in-depth interviews with eight experts in these fields. A line-by-line analysis of their insights revealed subthemes rooted in sociocultural, economic, and intercultural dynamics.

Further coding uncovered themes connected to governance, democratic participation, and fatherhood responsibility. These findings suggest a gender justice lens is essential for civil society and global institutions to implement integrated programs that bridge gaps left by government systems.

Ultimately, the research points to a link between a girl's ability to access her rights and how her community responds to social progress. Advancing gender justice can reshape local and global communities—strengthening them socially, economically, and politically.

You've developed and managed teams of professionals, board members, and volunteers in 15 countries. What are the characteristics you seek in a team, and how do you get them aligned with your organization's mission?

Experience showed that making a lasting difference in the lives of vulnerable girls requires a global network of volunteers from diverse professions. Passion remains essential—to endure obstacles, meet setbacks with resolve, and share in the moments of progress. Equally important is the ability to think clearly, collaborate within a team, and act independently with ethical responsibility toward the communities we serve.

Persistence, adaptability, and a commitment to evidence-based problem-solving are necessary. Integrity must be non-negotiable. Listening with intention and acting with care carry weight when lives are impacted. Mistakes carry consequences, and the responsibility to do no harm leaves little room for error.

Building a team of professionals who bring expertise, openness, and sound judgment is critical. A belief in lifelong learning and recognizing that every experience contributes to growth helps ground local education efforts. Trusting team members to apply their judgment and lead within their strengths is a part of this process. The work is always about the mission, never centered on any one person.

Consider the role of a conductor guiding an orchestra—each instrument offering a unique sound, contributing to a unified performance. The same applies to team leadership. When failure occurs, it provides space to reassess and evolve. New ideas emerge, offering direction for others down the line.

Education sharpened my leadership across cultures. Teaching master's-level university courses in nonprofit development and leadership allowed me to blend academic theory with real-world application, helping others craft practical tools to use in their own work.

Along with your nonprofit career, you've written children's books and educational resources. How do you view literature as an advocacy tool? What messages do you want to convey through your work?

Literature opened new ways of seeing the world. Hermann Hesse explored change as a constant force shaping life. *To Kill a Mockingbird* revealed, through Harper Lee's lens, the stark reality of injustice. Sylvia Plath gave language to the depths of depression. Each voice brought a new layer of understanding.

Mark Twain shaped my sense of humor and perspective. More than a humorist, he was a political thinker, writer, and traveler who used wit as both a tool and a mirror. His ability to speak truth through humor influenced my own approach to storytelling and life. I've read all of Twain's novels and reflections—his work was high on my reading list for years. I particularly love one of his quotes, "Life is short. Break the rules. Forgive quickly. Kiss slowly. Love truly. Laugh uncontrollably. And never regret anything that makes you smile."

My writing has ranged from children's stories to an internationally awarded romance novel, *Weep for Love*, which speaks to the idea of love as melody—something felt deeply and never out of reach. *Crystal Moonlight*, a book for children, encourages seeing with the heart more than the eyes. Each of my books carries pieces of my experience, woven into stories that reflect lessons I've lived.

The values I write about are clear: hold on to hope, see beyond appearances, stay curious, and pay attention to how people live, love, and express meaning in different ways. These themes guide not only my writing but how I choose to live and lead.

With many successes in public policy, nonprofit leadership, and education, how do you define success on a personal level? Looking back, is there one moment or achievement that stands out to you as your proudest?

There are lessons that have reshaped how I view success and the milestones I hold closest. I've walked across red-hot coals, jumped from a plane at 13,000 feet, earned a Ph.D., wrote an international award-winning romance novel, and spoke at the United Nations. I've worked with vulnerable girls in a former war zone and ran a half marathon at 63. Each of these moments holds a place in my memory.

But they were just that—moments. Markers of goals met, dreams once dismissed as unreachable. Hosting two radio shows and a television program on education brought unexpected opportunities. I interviewed government leaders from across the globe, as well as artists and authors, and found ways to build new collaborations through conversation.

I have lived with depression for much of my life—what felt like suffocating darkness—but I never stopped. I kept reaching for my dreams. Each one achieved gave me the strength to reach for another. The work with vulnerable children deepened with every step forward. And of all my experiences, the one that stays with me most is finding the person I share my life with—my partner, my friend, my love. I always believed we would find each other.

Every milestone fed the courage to chase the next one. If asked to offer advice, I would say this: persistence matters. Hope matters. Refusing to quit matters. Without those, none of what I've done would have come to pass.

To me, success means contributing to the life of a child—sharing knowledge, showing up, and making time. No single event stands above the others. Every accomplishment helped me grow into someone who could do a little more, give a little more, and help shape a more just world. In the Jewish tradition, *Tzedakah*—justice through giving—is how we repair the world, one act at a time.

I know it's impossible to sum up your entire journey in one answer, but if you had to start from scratch today, knowing everything you know now, how would you do it? In short, what's the single most valuable lesson you would share with aspiring entrepreneurs?

I immersed myself in spiritual literature by thinkers like Emmanuel Kant, Florence Scovel Shinn, and Emmet Fox, searching for answers. At one point, pursuing a career in education seemed fleeting, as negative automatic thoughts clouded my mind and made me lose sight of what truly mattered. Despite this, my determination to persevere remained constant. The answer came to me early, as a young adult reading *Siddhartha* by Hermann Hesse. In it, Hesse writes that life is like a river, constantly flowing and changing. I embraced that metaphor, becoming a river of change myself, learning, experiencing, and staying in the flow of life.

The secret to navigating this journey is simple yet profound: hold on to hope because it grounds you in the present, and give yourself permission to change and grow. I couldn't teach children the importance of persistence and resilience if I wasn't living proof of those values.

Through my experiences, I came to understand that ethical and moral values, hope, and perseverance—combined with those moments of unexpected insight—shaped me. I cultivated a young mindset, constantly learning, and found comfort in the gift of words. This allowed me to grow into someone more mindful, self-aware, and spiritually conscious, understanding that I am more than just the sum of my parts.

Surprisingly, chronic depression and my struggles led me to develop empathy, particularly as I became acutely aware of the educational disparities facing girls in poverty.

I made a vow never to give up. In a letter to his brother Theo, Vincent Van Gogh wrote, "Within the depth of depression that takes over my mind, is a place where harmony and music have a safe refuge. This enabled me to search for beauty in everything. That is what I paint."

Over time, years of sadness gave way to wisdom. I began to see that living an ethical life is simple in theory but far more challenging in practice. Ethics are shaped by culture—by what is deemed acceptable behavior. Morality, on the other hand, is passed down through generations, from parent to child. For me, living a Jewish life is rooted in the belief in oneself. To offer love to others, you must first have something to give.

Hillel the Elder, a Jewish scholar, once said, "If I am not for myself, who will be for me? But if I am only for myself, what am I? And if not now, when?"

Empathy, forged in my own struggles, helped me see others' challenges more clearly. Once I stopped defining myself by my sadness, I began to recognize the untapped potential within myself and others.

As Thornton Wilder wrote, "We all know that something is eternal. And it ain't houses, and it ain't names, and it ain't earth, and it ain't even the stars... everybody knows in their bones that something is eternal and that something has to do with human beings. All the greatest people who ever lived have been telling us that for five thousand years and yet you'd be surprised how people are always losing hold of it. There's something way down deep that's eternal about every human being.

Key Takeaways

- Setbacks Ignite Purpose: Math derailed his pre-med attempt, and David shifted into education, having a Ph.D. by 40. Sponsorship of a Thai girl led to the founding of To Love Children. Failure doesn't kill you; it directs you where you need to glow.
- Epiphanies Direct Action: A Thailand village walk struck close to home—girls required schools, not sympathy. In 2005, he had funded 50. One spark can ignite a mission if you do, rather than dream.
- Empathy Drives Change: Depression showed him the weight of pain, and he looked into a Kenyan girl's eyes and sponsored her class. Theory isn't what drives lasting change, it's compassion.
- Harmony Connects: Heading 15 nations, he coordinated teachers and donors like a conductor; U.N. status

followed next. A Zambian school opened in '18. Harmony transforms individual notes into lasting change.

- Hope Keeps Alive: He struggled through university and policy reports, but faithfulness kept him going. A female graduate in '22 validated: hope beats hopelessness with patient perseverance.
- Innovate From The Ground: Worldwide influence branched out from one Thai community; U.N. power scaled up, not initiated. Small victories, such as educating 100 girls in 2010, illustrate tangible changes established in the local area before expansion.

FROM STAGE TO STRATEGY WITH ENDURANCE AND LEADERSHIP

By Nick Day

Meet our next groundbreaker, Nick Day, whose stage lights dimmed when theatre debts pushed him into the world of Payroll and HR Recruitment. He established JGA Recruitment during the 2008 economic crisis, as business salaries remained largely unaffected by economic downturns. He utilized his practical skills to develop a thriving business that combined authentic relationships with a refusal to wait for calm waters. His rigorous swimming, cycling, and running initiatives taught him how to develop endurance, which helped him navigate technological changes and global business pressures. No script, just a steady climb from shaky ground to solid leadership. Through this chapter, Nick demonstrates how uncertainty, combined with guts and pacing, transformed what started as an unexpected diversion into a lasting victory, proving that achievement develops through steadfast and unending progress.

Nick, you have an incredibly diverse background. From an MA in Theatre and Performance to becoming a globally recognixed payroll and HR recruitment leader, what inspired your transition into this industry? How do you think your journey shaped your approach to business?

In 2002, having just completed an MA in Theatre and Performance at Royal Holloway, University of London, I would have laughed if someone told me I'd become a leader in payroll and HR recruitment. My career shift wasn't part of a grand plan—it was driven by the need to pay off university debt. The dream of a career in theatre clashed with the reality of financial stability, so I turned to a sector focused on people. I joined a recruitment firm specializing in payroll and HR with little knowledge of the industry, but my passion for performance and people quickly translated from the stage to the sales floor.

Recruitment, I realized, wasn't that different from theatrical storytelling. Every candidate had a story shaped by their experiences, and every company had its own narrative. My role was to align these stories, matching talent with opportunity. Within two years, I became a director—not because I mastered payroll, but because I understood people, what drives them, and how to place them in the right environments.

In 2008, I took a significant leap and launched JGA Recruitment, even though the global financial crisis was in full swing. Businesses were cutting budgets, and the recruitment industry was struggling. However, payroll remained non-negotiable; businesses still needed skilled professionals to handle it. This insight, supported by an investor who would become my mentor, helped us navigate the challenges and build a successful enterprise.

Over the years, I've learned two key principles. First, resilience is crucial. Whether an actor facing rejection or an entrepreneur navigating tough times, success comes from perseverance and adaptability. Second, success is rooted in human connection. In theatre, recruitment, or leadership, it's not about what you sell but how you make people feel. My career hasn't been defined by filling vacancies but by helping people find roles that transform their lives and supporting businesses in finding the talent that drives success.

Reflecting on my journey, I see that my transition from theatre to payroll recruitment was not a departure but an evolution. The storytelling, emotional intelligence, and understanding of human motivation I developed in theatre have been integral to the success of JGA Recruitment.

Setting up a specialised recruitment agency entails specific challenges. What were the greatest challenges you experienced when scaling JGA Recruitment, and how did you overcome them?

When I launched JGA Recruitment in 2008, I aimed to build a specialist firm that would compete in the payroll and HR recruitment industry and redefine it. I also wanted to elevate the profile of these fields by giving them a voice. What I didn't expect was the scale of challenges involved in scaling the business.

Starting the company was difficult, but scaling it required a shift in mindset, leadership, infrastructure, and culture. The lessons learned along the way have helped JGA become a respected leader in payroll and HR recruitment.

Despite the global financial crisis, I saw an opportunity. Payroll is essential—businesses still need to pay employees, regardless of the economy. I've always believed that success is possible in any market with a clear vision and determination. There's rarely a perfect time to start anything, as I learned when I became a father in 2009. Growth often comes from adversity.

Launching JGA during a challenging economic period laid a strong foundation for the future. We focused on our niche, specializing in payroll recruitment when others were generalists. This strategy, combined with relationship-building and a multi-channel approach, set us apart. We became the go-to experts in payroll, and our commitment to client partnerships helped sustain us.

In a competitive industry dominated by large firms, we knew we had to offer more than just filling vacancies. We adopted a consultative, value-driven approach, advising businesses on workforce trends and payroll challenges. Our thought leadership, through initiatives like *The Payroll Podcast* and *The HR L&D Podcast* and speaking at industry events, positioned us as trusted advisors rather than just recruiters.

One of the hardest lessons was learning that being a great recruiter doesn't automatically make you a great leader. In the early days, I did everything myself—client relationships, placements, operations, marketing. As we grew, I realized the importance of delegation. I shifted from being a top biller to a business leader, focusing on hiring the right people and building an organizational structure that could support growth. By investing in leadership development and fostering a culture of accountability, I empowered my team, allowing JGA to thrive as a collective effort.

As we scaled, we recognized the need for technology to maintain efficiency while keeping our personal touch. We embraced innovation, adopting new solutions to meet the future needs of businesses, and thought leadership kept us at the forefront of industry discussions.

In hindsight, our journey has been shaped by focus—focusing on what matters most, building expertise, empowering our team, and investing in scalable technology. Each challenge we faced taught us valuable lessons. Success, I've realized, means doing what matters with authenticity, continuous reflection, and a relentless drive to improve.

Your company was recognised as a *Great Place to Work* in 2023 and 2024. What specific cultural philosophies have helped create a thriving workplace environment?

Being named a *Great Place to Work* in 2023 and 2024 affirmed what we'd been building since day one: a culture rooted in trust, autonomy, and purpose. For me, culture isn't defined by perks or team-building days. It's how people feel when they show up. Do they feel valued? Heard? Do they believe their work matters?

At JGA Recruitment, we set out to build a company where people want to work, not just where they're expected to be. Our culture rests on three principles: Collaboration, Consistency, and Care. These guide everything from hiring to decision-making.

Collaboration drives our success. Recruitment often encourages individual competition, but we chose a team-first approach. Wins are shared. Knowledge is passed on. Our consultants support and challenge each other. This creates a high-performing, connected environment.

Consistency builds trust. While many companies promote values, few uphold them. We make sure our principles show up in every interaction and decision. No matter how long someone's been with us, they experience stable leadership, support, and fairness.

Care is our foundation. I remind myself and others often to "be more kind." Everyone is navigating something. That mindset shapes our leadership style. It's not just about results—it's about people.

Recruitment is a high-pressure industry. Targets and commissions drive performance, and burnout is common. At JGA Recruitment, we've worked intentionally to ensure that high pressure doesn't define our environment. We focus on well-being, flexibility, and building a psychologically safe workplace. People do their best work when they feel genuinely supported.

A key part of this is autonomy. We trust our team to manage their time and focus on outcomes, not hours. Whether through remote work, flexible schedules, or encouraging regular breaks, we empower people to work in ways that suit them. We also provide healthy breakfast and lunch options, letting employees choose what's stocked—always organic and sustainably packaged.

Growth is another focus. We believe in continuous learning and challenge. Through mentorship, external training, and coaching, our team has a clear path to advance and expand their skills. A strong culture doesn't just make people comfortable—it helps them evolve.

Recognition also plays a vital role. We celebrate wins, both big and small. Whether it's a new placement or someone going the extra mile, we make sure contributions are seen and valued.

Our culture is built on diversity, inclusion, and psychological safety. We create space for people to bring their full selves to work—whether they're dealing with personal challenges or celebrating life events. Regular employee-led groups support well-being, encourage dialogue, and keep us accountable to real-time feedback.

Our recognition as a *Great Place to Work* wasn't luck. It came from consistently leading with values. By committing to collaboration, consistency, and care, we've built a workplace where people feel safe, respected, and motivated to thrive.

With decades in payroll, you have seen tremendous changes in technology, compliance, and workforce demands. What are the biggest transformations you've seen in the industry? How has JGA Recruitment adapted to these shifts?

Over the past 20 years, payroll has shifted from a transactional back-office task to a strategic part of business operations. It now impacts compliance, employee well-being, global workforce management, and technology integration. At JGA Recruitment, adapting to this evolution has been key to staying ahead in a fast-changing industry.

One of the most impactful changes has been the rise of automation and AI. When I began, payroll was mostly manual—spreadsheets, legacy systems, and repetitive data entry were the norm. Mistakes were common, and compliance risks were high. Today, AI enables real-time processing, predictive compliance, and seamless integration with finance and HR systems. Payroll has become a valuable source of insight and strategy.

This evolution has brought a new demand: payroll professionals who understand both compliance and technology. With automation handling routine tasks, there's a growing need for skills in data analysis, system integration, regulatory knowledge, and employee experience. We've reshaped our hiring strategies to reflect this shift, focusing on professionals who can navigate complexity and innovation.

Globalization has also transformed payroll. As companies expand internationally, payroll has grown more complex, requiring the navigation of diverse tax laws, compliance rules, and reporting standards. Accurate, timely payments across borders demand specialized expertise. In response, we've developed global payroll talent networks to help multinational firms find professionals who understand international regulations and cross-border workforce needs. We've also worked to educate companies on the importance of treating global payroll as a strategic priority.

Another major shift is payroll's role in employee well-being. It now extends beyond timely payment to include how and when people are paid. Flexible pay options, earned wage access, and real-time payments are increasingly common, giving employees greater control over their finances. Payroll professionals are now key contributors to financial wellness and engagement strategies, directly influencing a company's ability to attract and retain talent.

These developments have reshaped the talent landscape. Companies now seek payroll leaders who understand compliance, systems, benefits, and employee experience. At JGA Recruitment, we've adapted by finding candidates who can connect payroll to broader HR and wellbeing initiatives.

All of this has raised payroll's profile. Once seen as a back-office function, it now plays a critical role in workforce planning, talent retention, and business strategy. Payroll errors now impact trust, morale, and brand reputation.

Today, demand for roles like payroll directors, heads of transformation, and strategic consultants has surged. Many of these positions didn't exist a decade ago, but organizations now recognize the importance of payroll leadership. I'm proud JGA Recruitment has helped place professionals driving this change.

Looking ahead, innovation will continue to shape the industry. AI, blockchain, and real-time processing will redefine operations while compliance and employee expectations evolve. What's clear is that payroll has become a strategic force companies can't afford to overlook.

You were ranked the #1 Global Thought Leader in Payroll and #9 in HR by Thinkers360. What do you believe makes your insights different, and how do you maintain a leadership edge in this industry that's always moving?

The accolades are great, but they didn't happen overnight. I've worked to elevate payroll and HR beyond their transactional roots—writing articles, contributing to industry publications, hosting webinars and roundtables, and launching two podcasts—all to spotlight their vital role in organizational success.

Payroll professionals often manage one of the largest financial responsibilities in a business, yet they're frequently viewed as technical rather than strategic. Similarly, HR is sometimes undervalued as administrative rather than as a driver of culture and transformation. My work has focused on challenging these misperceptions and reinforcing their influence on recruitment, retention, engagement, and long-term performance. Companies that overlook this strategic importance risk losing their edge—and their people.

A key part of staying relevant has been constant learning and adaptation. I regularly engage with global industry leaders, conduct ongoing research, and use my platform to raise awareness of emerging challenges. Over the past decade, I've completed two MA-level qualifications—one in professional consulting and another in executive coaching—along with an AI for Business Leaders certification to stay ahead of technological shifts.

This commitment fuels my push for change. Payroll and HR should be proactive forces, not reactive responders. I advocate for payroll leaders to have a voice in strategic planning and digital transformation and for HR professionals to shape culture and innovation, not just policy. Leadership in these areas means having the courage to challenge assumptions—and the insight to lead what comes next.

Authenticity has always been central to my approach. People respond to real stories—not jargon or abstract forecasts. My path from a theatre degree to leading a payroll and HR recruitment firm shapes how I communicate. I talk openly about what works, what doesn't, and the lessons learned from both. Whether it's the challenges of hiring the right talent or the missed potential in undervaluing payroll's role, I focus on sharing insights that are grounded, relatable, and useful.

Staying active within the global payroll and HR community keeps my perspective sharp. Hosting *The Payroll Podcast*, *The HR L&D Podcast*, and *Mindful Paths* gives me the chance to learn from top leaders in every conversation. These exchanges surface new trends, evolving practices, and technologies reshaping the workplace. I learn alongside thousands of listeners, all gaining from the perspectives of expert guests.

Outside the studio, I speak at conferences, write for industry publications, and collaborate with tech providers to better understand how digital tools are transforming payroll and HR. I don't just report on change—I help drive it.

More than anything, I believe thought leadership should lead to action. I work with businesses to improve payroll systems, support HR leaders in shaping inclusive cultures, and help companies hire talent aligned with their future goals. Real leadership means translating insights into results.

I also urge the next generation of leaders to stay curious—keep asking what's next and be open to the answers. That mindset keeps me motivated and fuels the conversations I lead.

In 2024, I was honored to receive the Global Vision Award from PayrollOrg, alongside recognition as an EMEA Top Voice and a leading global voice in payroll and HR. While I'm proud of these acknowledgments, the real achievement is helping professionals think differently, lead with clarity, and keep pace with a world that never stops changing.

As the author of *The Future of Payroll: How AI is Revolutionising the Industry*, what is the most exciting (or concerning) development you foresee in payroll automation?

When I wrote that ebook in 2024, my goal was to explore how artificial intelligence and automation are transforming payroll—while acknowledging the risks that come with rapid change. Once viewed as a back-office necessity, payroll is now a key driver of digital innovation. AI is changing how payroll is processed and how companies manage compliance, workforce planning, and financial well-being.

The biggest shifts include real-time payroll processing, employee self-service, and predictive analytics. Where payroll once ran on fixed cycles and lagged in correcting errors, AI now enables instant processing that accounts for real-time tax changes, overtime, and deductions. This reduces mistakes and gives employees greater control over their pay, which has improved satisfaction and financial security across the board.

Compliance, long a complex challenge due to constantly shifting regulations, is also being redefined. AI tools track global changes and update systems automatically, easing the burden on teams and reducing the risk of fines and errors—especially for multinational companies.

Machine learning is opening new insights into payroll data. Rather than simply issuing payments, payroll is emerging as a powerful lens into business operations. AI-driven analytics can flag risks like turnover, unexpected labor costs, and even payroll fraud, helping leaders make smarter, data-informed decisions.

Still, the shift comes with challenges. Over-reliance on automation can cause problems when human oversight is removed. AI can't replicate human empathy or judgment—especially when dealing with sensitive payroll queries, complex compliance questions, or nuanced workforce decisions. Governance matters, and without it, mistakes may go unnoticed, or employees may feel ignored.

There's also concern about job displacement. As the founder of JGA Recruitment, I've spoken with many professionals who are anxious about automation. But the reality is that AI is not replacing payroll roles—it's reshaping them. Automation will reduce repetitive tasks, freeing payroll professionals to focus on strategy, insight, and leadership. The future belongs to those who can integrate AI with human expertise.

AI is here to stay and will continue to reshape payroll, but success will depend on how thoughtfully businesses adopt it. With the right balance between technology and human insight, this era could mark the most meaningful transformation the payroll profession has ever seen—and I believe it will.

With *The Payroll Podcast, The HR L&D Podcast,* and the *Mindful Paths Podcast,* plus keynote speeches worldwide, what key lessons have you learned about engaging audiences and shaping industry discourse?

Engaging audiences has been one of the most fulfilling parts of my career. Speaking, podcasting, and presenting have given me a platform to influence industry thinking, challenge assumptions, and start conversations that matter. These moments also connect back to my early roots in theatre—reminding me that powerful communication begins with connection and belief in the possibility of change. I aim to build that through storytelling, enthusiasm for payroll and HR, and content that delivers lasting value.

One of the most important lessons I've learned is that people respond to authenticity. Whether I'm speaking to a large crowd or recording a podcast, the moments that stick are the unscripted, honest ones. Audiences aren't looking for sales pitches or perfect answers—they want real experiences, open conversations, and genuine reflection. That's why I avoid jargon and focus instead on what truly matters to professionals on the ground. The best talks feel like conversations, even when I'm the only one speaking.

I've also learned the impact of storytelling. Data matters, but it doesn't move people unless it's tied to a story they can relate to. A case of a payroll error that cost millions or an HR leader transforming workplace culture carries more weight than a slide full of statistics. Stories stick. They create emotional connections that make insights memorable—and useful.

A third key insight: relevance and adaptability are crucial for engagement. No single message works for every audience. A payroll manager in London will have different needs than one in Texas. A startup's HR lead faces different pressures than an enterprise-level executive. Knowing your audience and adjusting your message to fit their needs keeps engagement real and meaningful.

Before any keynote, I research my audience: their biggest challenges, current industry trends, and what they need to hear. Engagement comes from tailoring content, not delivering a one-size-fits-all message. I never approach a talk as someone with all the answers. People want perspective, not perfection. Mine is shaped by working with payroll and HR leaders globally, not as a practitioner but as a recruiter with a broader lens. That distance gives me insight others might miss—and it's helped shape my evolution as a speaker and podcast host. I'm especially proud that *The Payroll Podcast* is now the most listened-to show in its field worldwide.

One lesson I didn't expect to learn is how essential curiosity is in thought leadership. Hosting *The Payroll Podcast* and *The HR L&D Podcast* has connected me with CEOs, policymakers, authors, and innovators. The best interviews don't come from showing what you know but from asking the right questions. What makes this guest's view unique? What hasn't been said yet? What will stretch the audience's thinking? Real insight comes from conversation, not from certainty.

Another major lesson is the importance of consistency. Thought leadership is built over time, not through a single keynote or hit podcast episode. When I launched *The Payroll Podcast* in 2018 and *The HR L&D Podcast* in 2019, I had no idea whether they would succeed. Through steady effort and ongoing relevance, both have become trusted resources. The same is true of public speaking—real impact comes through repetition, growth, and showing up again and again.

I've come to understand that people want more than just information—they want inspiration and practical insights they can use. Before I take the mic, I ask myself: Will this solve a problem? Will it challenge someone to think differently? Will it leave them better equipped to succeed? If so, I've done what I set out to do.

At its core, engagement is about creating impact—sparking new ideas, shifting perspectives, and giving people something they can carry forward. Whether through podcasts, keynotes, or panels, my mission remains the same: to elevate the conversation and help payroll and HR professionals lead with confidence.

Beyond payroll, you're an ILM Level 7 Qualified Executive Coach. What are some common leadership challenges that payroll and HR executives face, and how do you help them work through these issues?

Leadership in payroll and HR presents distinct challenges. These fields operate at the intersection of compliance, finance, and human capital, demanding a balance of regulatory precision and strategic decision-making. Payroll leaders ensure accuracy in financial processes, while HR executives drive cultural transformation, talent retention, and workforce engagement. As an ILM Level 7 Qualified Executive Coach, I've worked with many leaders to help them navigate these complexities. This led me to launch T4M Coaching Ltd, where I provide coaching services focused on promoting transformational change.

A major challenge for leaders is overcoming imposter syndrome. Payroll and HR have often been seen as support functions and undervalued in executive discussions, despite payroll managing significant costs and HR shaping workplace culture. This underappreciation contributes to feelings of imposter syndrome, so much of my coaching focuses on helping leaders recognize their strategic value.

Coaching is transformational in this context. I work with leaders to shift their mindset and understand that their contributions are vital to business success. Payroll and HR professionals maintain employee trust, financial integrity, and compliance stability—without them, businesses fail. When leaders internalize this, their confidence grows, and they begin to have a greater impact in executive settings.

My coaching helps leaders reposition themselves as business influencers rather than functional experts. For instance, payroll leaders aren't just responsible for paying employees; they have insights into workforce costs, overtime, and compliance risks that affect profitability. Similarly, HR executives shape retention strategies that reduce turnover and boost productivity. I guide leaders to communicate their value in ways that resonate with CEOs and CFOs.

Coaching also supports leaders in developing a proactive mindset. Payroll and HR executives often face challenges like economic downturns, regulatory changes, and workforce disruptions. During the COVID-19 pandemic, payroll leaders ensured furlough schemes and government subsidies were executed correctly, while HR redefined remote work policies and prioritized employee wellbeing.

A key lesson in my coaching is the importance of staying calm under pressure. Leaders often overreact or freeze during crises, which can hinder effective decision-making. I help them develop strategies to assess risks quickly and lead with clarity and confidence.

Balancing operational demands with strategic leadership remains a challenge. Payroll and HR leaders often focus on day-to-day tasks, leaving little time for broader thinking. Coaching helps leaders delegate effectively, develop future leaders, and create space for strategic work. The most successful executives empower their teams, make high-impact decisions, and lead with clarity and vision.

Ultimately, outstanding leadership requires expertise, adaptability, and the ability to drive change. Through coaching, I help leaders build confidence, expand their influence, and lead with authority and authenticity.

From competing in the Ironman World Championships to placing 3rd in the Obstacle Course World Championships, you push your limits beyond business. How do endurance sports influence your leadership style and decision-making?

Athletic endurance challenges and leadership principles are deeply connected. My journey through Obstacle Course Racing and Ironman competitions has been a catalyst for personal growth, strategic thinking, and resilience.

In 2015, during the Obstacle Course World Championships in Ohio, a competitor told me I didn't belong there, and the results seemed to confirm his doubt. I finished far down the rankings, but those words fueled me. The next year, I turned that setback into a triumph, earning a bronze medal in the Blue Mountains of Canada. It took a year of focused training, improving weaknesses, and committing to the goal. Standing on that podium draped in the Union Jack was more than a victory—it was proof of the power of persistent improvement.

In 2021, I set myself a new challenge: breaking the 10-hour Ironman time barrier. An Ironman includes a 3.8km swim, 180km bike ride, and a 42.2km marathon. I completed my first Ironman in Zurich in 2012 with a time of 10:45:25. Now, at 39, I aimed to cut over 45 minutes off my time, a goal many thought impossible given my age and the demands of being a CEO, husband, and father.

One coach initially refused to work with me, doubting my ability to balance training with my busy life. But his skepticism only fueled my determination. I found another coach who believed in my potential. The training was grueling: 5:00 am bike rides, late-night swims, and running at every opportunity. I sacrificed time with family and friends, even playing poker over Zoom while riding a Wattbike for a 5-hour endurance session. The support of my family was crucial to this journey.

In 2022, I completed my goal with a 9:56:27 time in Estonia, crossing the finish line to the cheers of my family. Along the way, I qualified for the Ironman 70.3 World Championships in Utah by finishing 5th in Staffordshire. By 2023, I was ranked the 10th best British athlete in my age group and earned the Ironman All-World Athlete Gold Award.

These achievements are more than athletic milestones; they are lessons in leadership and growth. Success isn't instantaneous—it's the result of months or even years of incremental improvements. It requires structured routines, consistent effort, and an unwavering commitment to showing up, even when motivation wanes. These principles apply just as much in business as they do in sports.

Every race presents a moment of intense challenge, typically in the final stretch of an Ironman marathon or halfway through a muddy obstacle race. It's when your body screams to quit, and your mind must take control. These moments test mental resilience. Do you slow down or push through the discomfort?

During Ironman Estonia, I faced doubt, but I achieved my sub-10-hour goal with less than four minutes to spare. The same happens in business, where unexpected challenges test our resolve. We often find our potential when we lean into fear and push through adversity.

Leadership and entrepreneurship demand tough decisions under pressure. When obstacles arise, the instinct is to retreat, but exceptional leaders embrace discomfort, knowing that adversity is essential to growth.

Endurance taught me that success isn't about constant effort but strategic energy management. In an Ironman, sprinting from the start leads to failure. You must pace yourself, knowing when to push and when to conserve energy. Similarly, in business, constant full-capacity work leads to burnout. Success lies in knowing when to accelerate and when to recover.

Adaptability is key. No race or business plan goes as expected. A puncture, unexpected weather, or sudden injury may require adjustments. The best performers stay calm, assess the situation, and pivot without losing sight of the goal. This mindset shapes my leadership at JGA Recruitment, where we don't expect perfection but strive for agility in facing challenges.

Though endurance sports seem individual, success relies on a support network of coaches, training partners, family, and friends. Leadership follows the same principle. No entrepreneur succeeds alone, so surrounding yourself with the right people is vital.

The real competition is against yourself. The goal is continuous growth—becoming a better version of yourself each day. This mindset drives both my endurance and business approach. Success is about improvement, not comparison.

In sports and business, the journey matters more than the finish line. Endurance sports have shaped me into a leader who thrives under pressure, turns obstacles into opportunities, and knows that success comes from having the strength and discipline to go the distance while enjoying the ride.

I know it's impossible to sum up your entire journey in one answer, but if you had to start from scratch today, knowing everything you know now, how would you do it? In short, what's the single most valuable lesson you would share with aspiring individuals like you?

My entrepreneurial journey started in recruitment, an industry I knew but had yet to shape through my own vision. When I launched JGA Recruitment, there was no clear blueprint for success. What I did have was a readiness to embrace uncertainty, confidence in my abilities, and a commitment to show up, no matter the challenge.

Many aspiring entrepreneurs wait for the "perfect moment," but I've learned you'll never feel fully ready. Action creates opportunity and clarity, so take that first step. If you have an idea and the drive to turn it into reality, don't wait—act now.

If you're unsure how to proceed, focus on the "who." Who in your network—mentors, colleagues, or friends—can help you accelerate your growth? Surround yourself with people who challenge and inspire you. Their insights will help guide your next move.

Failure is an unavoidable part of the journey. The key difference between those who succeed and those who don't is how they respond to it. Every setback is another step forward. Learn quickly, trust yourself, and keep pushing, even after a failure.

The road won't always be smooth, but if you approach each step with commitment and curiosity, you'll adapt and succeed. The most important lesson I've learned is that when fear arises, it's a signal to lean into it. That's where growth happens, transforming uncertainty into opportunity. Take those courageous steps, and you'll find your path.

Key Takeaways

- Action Beats Timing: Nick founded JGA Recruitment during the 2008 economic downturn when hiring ground to a halt and budgets contracted. Payroll was a lifeline; individuals still required paychecks, regardless of the crisis. Launching then wasn't perfect, but holding off would have set everything back. It's a reminder: opportunity lurks in disruption if you act rather than overthink.
- Niche Wins Big: Betting everything on payroll recruitment was not glamorous but intelligent. Whereas others struggled to be generalists amid a competitive industry, Nick fixed his sights on a critical, underappreciated niche. And that specificity whittled down a reputation and loyal customers who demonstrated intense specialized knowledge, as opposed to shotgun attempts to hit a bull's-eye.
- People Over Process: His theatre days taught him that connection is more important than transactions. At JGA, he established a team culture built on trust and shared

successes rather than just goals. As a *Great Place to Work*, it's proof that people-centricity, beyond filling seats, provides a foundation that stands the test of time.

- Ironman molds leadership: 3.8 km swim, 180 km bike, 42.2 km run. Ironman races duplicate business marathons. A sub-10-hour finish in Estonia was achieved through pacing rather than sprinting and overcoming exhaustion. Nick operates in a consistent, calculated, and prepared manner, focusing on the long term rather than just the short term.
- Adapt or Fade: Payroll Transitions from Spreadsheets to AI and the Growing Complexity of Global Operations. Nick did not cling to traditional practices; instead, he was not hesitant to adopt technology and trends, creating networks to meet the requirements of multinational companies. Stagnation is death; adapting with purpose keeps you current and ahead.
- Fear Fuels Growth: From theatre to recruitment, a bronze medal after a weak race, a crisis-born business—Nick leaned into doubt every time. Each leap past fear unlocked new strength, showing that potential lives just beyond discomfort if you're willing to step up.

"TURNING TRAUMA INTO TRIUMPH" HOW TO EMBRACE RESILIENCE

By Kenya Lee

Say hello to Kenya Lee, whose world shattered when she was 23 weeks pregnant, losing her daughter Faith to an abusive relationship, only to find her calling in the wreckage. Her 20-year nursing career led her to found Faith In Girls Inc., through which she merged emotional recovery with monetary growth. Kenya utilizes The Path to Emotional Greatness and The Trinity Strategy to support women, employing Detroit rent-to-own homes in conjunction with her Trinity Strategy, which encompasses mindset, mastery, and action. She transforms scars from her trauma into tools for guidance and healing. She maintains professionalism in her scrubs while actively participating in her movement because she understands that difficulty brings meaningful reasons for existence. She explains in this chapter how her strength, combined with self-understanding, transformed her loss into a decisive tool to support others, demonstrating that success emerges from creating development out of hardship as a personal journey.

You have dedicated your life to empowering women and young girls through Faith In Girls, Inc. Can you share the defining moment or realization that led you to establish this organization, and how your personal journey shaped its mission?

I have experienced a few "wake-up calls" during my life, times when you are granted an opportunity to define or enhance your life's purpose. The major life event that forced me to redefine my life was when I found myself 23 weeks pregnant and involved in an abusive relationship. I had been letting life live me instead of living life. I had no value for myself and had no clue of my life's purpose; however, I am a believer that if we don't put forth any effort to figure the important things out, life has a way of doing it for us and presenting situations that give us no choice. This is what happened to me when I went into labor at 23 weeks gestation after arguing with my then-boyfriend. I rushed to the hospital full of fear after my water burst when it was surely much too early for me to have my baby. After being examined, I was told that my child had a 90% chance of being stillborn. Nevertheless, I would have to do the seemingly impossible by enduring labor and delivering the baby. Ten hours passed as I labored during childbirth, feeling as if it was in vain if my baby wouldn't be able to survive this strenuous labor.

When the 10 hours were over, my worst thought became a reality, and she was born without breath in her lungs. What a realization that the life I had been leading wasn't serving me. It was causing me harm and suffering that could have been avoided if did something about my circumstances and embraced change. I held my tiny, lifeless girl in my arms. She was so pure. So beautiful, so perfect. This tragedy shook me to my core; at that moment, I knew I was meant to contribute something meaningful to the world. I had been awakened by the loss of life, the life that could have been but wasn't. Her short presence to the world couldn't be in vain! I named her "Faith." Years later, I found an organization that would help women like me understand the "wake-up calls," process the trauma, and emerge to have a healthier and more productive life.

Starting a nonprofit and balancing it with a career in nursing is no easy feat. What were some of the biggest challenges you faced when launching Faith In Girls, and how did you navigate those obstacles?

One of the biggest challenges in launching Faith In Girls was securing the initial funding to bring our vision to life. Like many grassroots organizations, we had to be strategic in finding financial resources to purchase homes, develop programs, and support the women we serve. We overcame this by leveraging city programs, such as Detroit's low-cost home purchase initiative, applying for grants, and engaging with donors who believed in our mission. Every dollar was maximized to ensure long-term sustainability.

Another major hurdle was building trust within the community. Many of the women we serve have faced systemic barriers and housing instability, making it crucial to establish credibility. My personal experience—both professionally as a public health nurse and personally as someone who has overcome similar challenges—allowed me to connect with participants in a meaningful way. We prioritized transparency, hosted community engagement events, and ensured our programs addressed real, lived experiences.

Navigating bureaucracy was also a challenge, particularly when it came to acquiring homes, dealing with zoning laws, and ensuring legal compliance. We tackled this by forming strong relationships with city officials, legal experts, and community partners who helped us streamline processes and advocate for resources that benefit underserved women.

Sustaining and scaling our programs required thoughtful planning. We developed structured, evidence-based initiatives like *The Path to Egypt* online course and *The Path to Emotional Greatness* manual to provide both financial literacy and personal development support. Our rent-to-own housing program was also designed with long-term impact in mind, offering women a path to homeownership rather than temporary relief.

Your book, *The Path to Emotional Greatness*, and your work emphasize emotional well-being as a foundation for success. How do you believe emotional intelligence impacts a woman's ability to achieve financial independence and self-sufficiency?

Emotional intelligence is the foundation of financial independence and self-sufficiency, especially for women who have faced systemic barriers or personal hardships. Without self-awareness, resilience, and the ability to regulate emotions, it's difficult to make sound financial decisions, break cycles of instability, or navigate the challenges that come with building a secure future.

One of the most critical aspects of emotional intelligence is self-awareness—the ability to recognize how past experiences, fears, and behaviors influence financial choices. Many women have internalized limiting beliefs about money, success, and self-worth due to societal conditioning or personal setbacks. *The Path to Emotional Greatness* helps women identify these patterns and replace them with a mindset of abundance, self-belief, and strategic thinking. Another key factor is emotional regulation and resilience. Financial independence is a journey, often filled with setbacks. Women who can manage stress, overcome failures, and stay focused despite obstacles are more likely to persist in their goals—whether that's saving for a home, investing in education, or starting a business. Without emotional resilience, financial challenges can feel overwhelming, leading to avoidance or self-sabotaging behaviors.

Additionally, strong interpersonal skills and decision-making abilities—both core components of emotional intelligence—play a huge role in financial success. Negotiating salaries, setting boundaries around financial commitments, and making informed investment decisions all require confidence and clarity. Women who can communicate effectively, advocate for themselves, and build supportive networks are more likely to access opportunities for growth.

Through Faith In Girls, I've seen firsthand how emotional intelligence transforms financial behaviors. When women heal emotionally, they make better financial decisions, set long-term goals, and create stability for themselves and their families. By combining emotional well-being with financial literacy, we empower women not only to survive but truly thrive.

---

4. You developed The Trinity Strategy as a daily guide for overcoming trauma and gaining self-worth. Can you explain what makes this approach unique and share a powerful success story from someone who has applied it?

The Trinity Strategy emerged from my personal journey and years of working with women reclaiming their lives. This approach is unique because it focuses on three interconnected pillars: Mindset, Emotional Mastery, and Purposeful Action. It doesn't just involve healing from the past; it's also transforming pain into power and giving women the tools to achieve financial security, self-worth, and independence.

Mindset: Reprogramming the Narrative: Our thoughts shape our reality. Many women, especially those facing trauma or financial instability, carry subconscious beliefs that keep them in survival mode. They've been told they're not enough or that success is out of reach. The Trinity Strategy starts by reshaping these internal narratives. I guide women through exercises that replace negative self-talk with empowering beliefs, helping them align with their true potential.

Emotional Mastery: Healing Without Staying Stuck: Healing means processing past pain and learning to manage emotions. The Trinity Strategy teaches emotional regulation, mindfulness, and self-awareness to help women navigate stress, rejection, and uncertainty without self-sabotaging. Many women gain power simply by learning to manage their emotions rather than being controlled by them.

Purposeful Action: Moving with Intention Every Day: Healing requires action. For women coming from trauma, learning to trust themselves enough to take bold steps is crucial. The Trinity Strategy is practical, with women committing to small but intentional actions daily that align with their financial, personal, and career goals. Each step—whether setting boundaries, applying for jobs, or speaking kindly to themselves—builds confidence and momentum.

One of the most inspiring transformations I've witnessed was from a woman named Angela. When she came to Faith In Girls, she was in a cycle of financial instability, living paycheck to paycheck and feeling trapped in toxic relationships that reinforced her lack of self-worth. She had grown up in an environment where financial dependence was normalized, and despite being intelligent and driven, she didn't believe she could build something on her own.

Through The Trinity Strategy, Angela started with mindset work—challenging her beliefs about money, success, and relationships. She identified the core belief that had been holding her back: the idea that she was always meant to struggle. Once she rewrote that narrative, her confidence grew.

Next, she focused on Emotional Mastery. She had always reacted emotionally to financial stress—overspending when she felt anxious and avoiding tough conversations about money. By learning to regulate her emotions, she started making intentional financial decisions, setting goals instead of reacting impulsively.

Finally, she took Purposeful Action. She started saving—even if it was just $10 a week—because she had never believed she could before. She enrolled in financial literacy workshops, applied for better-paying jobs, and, most importantly, walked away from relationships that no longer aligned with her growth.

Fast forward to today, Angela is in the process of purchasing her first home through our rent-to-own program. She is thriving in a career she once thought was out of reach, and she no longer second-guesses her worth. What changed? It wasn't just financial education or healing from her past—it was The Trinity Strategy giving her the daily framework to bridge the gap between emotional well-being and tangible success.

This is why I do this work. The Trinity Strategy isn't just a method—it's a movement. When women heal, change their mindset, and take small but consistent steps toward their goals, their entire lives transform. And when one woman rises, she lifts an entire community with her.

From launching The Detroit Homeowner Program for Women to writing *The Path to Emotional Greatness*, your work spans different areas of empowerment. How do you balance these initiatives while ensuring they align with your core vision?

For me, balance means ensuring every initiative serves a unified mission. At the heart of Faith In Girls is the belief that empowerment grows from self-awareness, emotional intelligence, and financial security. Whether I'm helping a woman become a homeowner, guiding her through emotional healing, or teaching financial literacy, it all connects back to equipping women with the tools to transform their lives in lasting ways.

Before launching any project—a book, course, or program—I ask: Does this help women build emotional and financial independence? If it doesn't, I move on. That clarity keeps me from getting pulled into distractions that don't serve the mission. Emotional well-being and financial security aren't separate; they're deeply connected. I created The Path to E.G.Y.P.T. because I recognized how financial struggles often stem from emotional wounds, fear-based choices, or a lack of self-worth. Likewise, The Detroit Homeowner Program for Women is about more than housing—it builds confidence and life skills that support long-term success. By integrating emotional development into financial initiatives, each program strengthens the others.

Running multiple efforts requires structure and a team that shares the vision. I build systems—through mentorship, step-by-step curriculums, and strong partnerships—that help programs run smoothly. Still, I stay flexible, knowing true impact comes from meeting women where they are and adapting as needed.

I've also learned the importance of prioritization and delegation. I focus on where I can make the greatest difference—developing strategy, mentoring, and advocating for resources—while trusting my team to handle operations. That trust allows Faith In Girls to grow without burning out the people driving it forward.

Balancing all of this isn't always easy, but I stay grounded in my purpose. I've lived many of the same struggles as the women we serve, and that connection keeps me committed. I also protect time for self-care. Emotional mastery isn't just something I teach; it's how I stay centered and strong enough to keep going. Every book, every program, and every initiative is a reflection of that mission—helping women break cycles, heal, and build futures they're proud to claim.

As a registered nurse with over two decades of experience, how has your background in healthcare influenced the programs you've created for Faith In Girls? Do you see a link between emotional well-being and public health?

Absolutely. My background in healthcare has shaped the programs I've created for Faith In Girls. Working as a registered nurse for over 20 years—especially in underserved communities—has given me firsthand insight into how emotional well-being and public health are connected. Physical and financial struggles are often treated as separate issues, but they're usually rooted in emotional and psychological health.

As a nurse, I saw how trauma—whether from childhood adversity, poverty, or abusive relationships—affects both physical health and decision-making. Chronic stress can lead to conditions like hypertension, diabetes, and depression, but it also influences how women handle finances and stability. This is why Faith In Girls integrates emotional intelligence and trauma-informed practices into every program. When women begin to believe in their own worth, they start making choices that support long-term security.

In healthcare, I treated many women who were caught in cycles of financial instability that directly harmed their health. Some had to choose between paying rent or filling prescriptions, or stayed in unsafe relationships to survive financially. These stories inspired me to develop The Path to Emotional Greatness and The Trinity Strategy—approaches grounded in the idea that emotional resilience fuels financial independence. Our Detroit Homeowner Program reflects this belief, too. It's not just about housing; it's about ensuring women have the emotional and financial tools to sustain it.

Public health is about more than medicine—it's about stability, education, housing, and mental health. Without addressing these foundational needs, we're just treating symptoms. Faith In Girls takes a holistic approach, connecting self-awareness, financial empowerment, and community support to give women access to everything they need for long-term well-being.

There's a direct link between emotional well-being and public health. Women with strong emotional intelligence are more likely to make healthy choices, manage money wisely, leave harmful environments, and bounce back from adversity. Emotional wellness is a public health priority. When women are emotionally secure, they raise healthier children, build stronger communities, and contribute to broader economic stability. That's the vision behind Faith In Girls—helping individual women while creating generational change through emotional, financial, and community strength.

Being a leader in the nonprofit world comes with its own set of challenges. What leadership qualities have been most essential in your journey, and how do you continue to grow as a leader?

Leading in the nonprofit world means navigating uncertainty, inspiring change, and staying closely connected to the people you serve. My journey with Faith In Girls has required resilience, vision, and adaptability to turn challenges into opportunity.

One of the most important leadership tools I have is relatability. I've faced many of the same struggles as the women we serve—financial hardship, self-doubt, and the work of rebuilding after setbacks. That personal experience allows me to lead with authenticity and ensure that Faith In Girls remains rooted in real understanding, not abstract ideas.

Running a nonprofit means learning how to stretch limited resources. There are always funding gaps and systemic roadblocks. I've had to stay solution-focused—whether through securing grants, forming new partnerships, or reworking programs—to keep the focus on impact, not limitations.

Strong leadership requires long-term vision. From the beginning, I've built Faith In Girls with the goal of creating programs that change lives, not just offer temporary help. That means balancing strategy with daily execution and keeping every effort aligned with sustainable change.

The work is always evolving, so I stay open to learning. I attend leadership conferences, connect with other nonprofit leaders, and explore new tools and methods. Growth requires a willingness to adapt, and I welcome what helps us serve better.

Leadership is also about lifting others. I prioritize mentorship and help women within the organization grow into leadership roles themselves. By building strong teams and sharing responsibility, the mission becomes something bigger than one person's vision.

What keeps Faith In Girls moving forward is a commitment to the mission, a willingness to adjust when needed, and a focus on empowering others to lead. That's the kind of leadership that lasts.

One of your initiatives focuses on helping women secure housing despite financial barriers. What systemic challenges do you see in homeownership for women, and how does Faith In Girls help break these cycles?

Homeownership is a powerful step toward financial stability, yet many women—especially women of color—face deep systemic barriers that make this goal feel distant. Through Faith In Girls' Detroit Homeowner Program for Women, I've seen how historical inequities, financial challenges, and limited access to resources keep women from achieving lasting homeownership.

Women, particularly Black and minority women, have long been excluded from homeownership due to discriminatory lending, redlining, and wage gaps. These patterns persist, showing up in mortgage denial rates and higher borrowing costs. Financial barriers compound the issue. Single mothers and low-income earners often struggle with unstable employment and little generational wealth, making it hard to save for a down payment or secure a loan. Student debt and credit challenges further reduce access to affordable financing.

Even when homes are within reach, the path to ownership requires knowledge—understanding mortgages, budgeting for maintenance, and navigating the market. Too many women lack access to the kind of financial education that builds long-term readiness. Rising housing prices and stagnant wages shrink the window of opportunity, while gentrification and property taxes threaten to displace those who do manage to buy.

That's why our Detroit Homeowner Program helps women acquire city-owned properties through affordable, rent-to-own models. They build equity while gaining the skills and stability needed to transition into ownership. Our financial literacy workshops cover everything from budgeting to credit repair, giving women the tools to take charge of their financial future.

But we also know homeownership is more than a transaction. It's a shift in identity. Many women feel discouraged or unprepared, shaped by years of being told ownership isn't for them. Through The Path to Emotional Greatness and our mentorship programs, we work on mindset—building confidence, resilience, and a sense of possibility.

Support doesn't end at closing. We continue working with women to ensure they can sustain homeownership—offering education on home maintenance, access to local grants, and connections to a broader community. These pieces are essential to long-term success.

When women own homes, they create stability for their families and build assets that can be passed down. At Faith In Girls, we're not just helping women buy homes—we're helping them build futures rooted in strength, security, and generational wealth.

You've received prestigious recognitions, including the Los Angeles Global Impact Award and The Power of One Dedicated Woman Award. Looking ahead, what legacy do you hope to leave behind, and what new projects or goals are on the horizon for you?

I've always believed legacy isn't measured by awards or accolades but by lasting impact. My goal was never simply to create programs—it was to shift mindsets, break generational cycles, and help women claim ownership of their lives with confidence and stability. The legacy I hope to leave is one of empowerment and self-sufficiency, where women, especially those facing systemic barriers, are equipped with both emotional intelligence and financial tools to write new stories for themselves and their families.

I want to see a future where women aren't just surviving but building lives they're proud of. Their pasts don't define them. With the right support, they can own homes, heal from trauma, grow wealth, and lead with purpose. Through Faith In Girls, my aim is to leave behind a model that integrates emotional healing, financial literacy, and community into a framework for long-term success.

The Detroit Homeowner Program for Women is just the beginning. I'm working to scale this nationally, helping cities rethink how they support single mothers, underserved women, and first-time buyers—not with charity, but with sustainable pathways. Women are economic anchors in any community. Investing in them reduces poverty and fuels long-term growth.

Programs like The Path to Emotional Greatness and The Trinity Strategy go beyond personal development—they offer blueprints for how self-awareness and mindset lay the foundation for financial success. I want to see emotional intelligence taught alongside money management so women aren't just given advice but also the inner tools to apply it and sustain progress.

My next steps focus on scale and depth. I'm expanding the Detroit Homeowner Program beyond city limits through partnerships with municipalities, real estate leaders, and nonprofits. The goal is a national network that helps women transition from hardship to ownership through structured, supported models.

I'm also launching a mentorship and leadership accelerator designed for graduates of Faith In Girls to become mentors and advocates themselves—building a multiplying effect across communities. My next book explores the link between emotional well-being and financial independence, diving deeper into the strategies that have helped women transform their lives. I'll continue using national speaking platforms to share these ideas, pushing for policy shifts and broader inclusion in financial systems.

We're building a digital course and mentorship program to expand access to our financial empowerment model, making sure more women can benefit—no matter where they live.

Looking forward, I'm focused on building something that lasts. Systems, not just programs. Leaders, not just participants. A movement that continues without me, led by the women it was built for. The truest legacy I can leave isn't a title or recognition. It's women living fully, free from limitations, shaping a future they can pass on.

I know it's impossible to sum up your entire journey in one answer, but if you had to start from scratch today, knowing everything you know now, how would you do it? In short, what's the single most valuable lesson you have for women looking to grow their own initiatives?

Never give up on yourself. The world may not agree or even see your vision for success, but that cannot dictate your passion and purpose. We are all here to give our personal input. Never let anyone diminish what is yours.

Furthermore, never underestimate the power of emotional intelligence. Self-actualization is what will make you take the first step. Knowing how you work and how your body works is your biggest asset, and women who understand how to navigate circumstances through the assessment of themselves are the first ones to build their own initiatives.

If there's one thing I would tell women looking to build their own initiatives, it's this: don't wait for the perfect conditions—start where you are, with what you have, and trust that the path will reveal itself. The biggest difference between those who create impact and those who don't isn't knowledge or resources—it's the courage to begin, to keep going despite setbacks, and to trust that every step forward is shaping something greater than you can see in the moment.

Key Takeaways

- Pain Ignites Purpose: Kenya's stillbirth at 23 weeks, while being abused, wasn't simply a loss; it was a wake-up call. Giving her daughter the name Faith, she transformed her sorrow into purpose, establishing Faith In Girls to help women heal and rise. It's a study in deriving significance from adversity, refusing to let it define you.

- Healing Unlocks Wealth: She recognized emotional hurts, such as self-doubt or trauma, preventing financial stability in nursing patients. Her Trinity Strategy connects mindset changes to doable actions, such as Angela saving $10 a week to become a homeowner. Emotional intelligence is not a choice; it is the foundation of sustained independence.
- Small Wins Build Big Change: Beginning with Detroit's affordable homes, Kenya developed a rent-to-own plan in the face of financing difficulties. Incremental progress per woman housed, credit restoration, and a workshop snowball into disrupting poverty cycles. Impact does not require scale first; it requires intention.
- Health Fuels Empowerment: Twenty years of nursing work, years of trauma accompanied by decisions that didn't prioritize her well-being, proved to be stepping stones of accomplishing the life she deserved. Faith In Girls combines emotional skills with housing and literacy, addressing the social causes of health issues. Stable women build stable families, waves of influence rippling back into healthier communities.
- Resilience Overcomes Obstacles: Confronting bureaucracy and doubt, Kenya relied on empathy and determination to obtain grants and establish trust. Her flexibility, as she juggles nursing, writing, and leadership, demonstrates that resilience isn't fixed; it's a daily decision to move forward, regardless of the circumstances.
- Courage Starts It All: She didn't wait for perfect timing after the tragedy; she just began. Her advice to women, "Act now, trust your vision," reflects a life built on bold first steps. Success isn't about resources but the guts to move despite uncertainty.

BUILDING RESILIENT LEADERS: PSYCHOLOGY, STRENGTHS, AND SUSTAINABLE SUCCESS

By Ryan Crittenden

Introducing Ryan Crittenden, an Army vet turned Ph.D. who ditched fixing flaws for amplifying strengths. His supervisor's preoccupation with weaknesses led him to establish XL Coaching and Development to help organizations unlock their leadership potential. Ryan developed a science-based coaching method through his experience in military drills, psychology laboratories, and real estate transactions. He succeeded in overcoming "Mit," his impostor syndrome, which led him to develop a practice that transformed organizations by employing CliftonStrengths tools. According to him, the root cause of burnout emerges from mismatched effort rather than insufficient effort. This section demonstrates that sustaining success revolves around placing bets on your areas of expertise, which proves his concept of resilience involves growing more assertive rather than being perfect.

Ryan, your career path is remarkable, from being an Army veteran to earning a Ph.D. in Industrial and Organizational Psychology and becoming a strengths-based coaching leader. Can you share the defining moments that inspired you to establish XL Coaching and Development?

XL Coaching and Development was started with a passion to help leaders and their teams achieve clarity, motivation, and fulfillment in their personal and professional lives. I have seen those same things in my life, focusing on my strengths and how to grow, and I hope to do the same for others.

The most significant defining moment for getting into strengths-based leadership coaching came from my personal experience working with a leader who wanted to fix what he thought were weaknesses. Strengths-based leaders focus on who their people are and help them make a plan for success when the mission is outside of their strengths zone. People do not need to be fixed; they just need a community that knows and understands who they are and are not while affirming them.

How does a strength-based approach toward entrepreneurship transform leaders and businesses, and what common misconceptions do people have about building upon their strengths?

A strengths-based approach to entrepreneurship emphasizes identifying and leveraging individual and team strengths, leading to enhanced performance and job satisfaction. By focusing on what individuals do best, leaders can foster a more engaged and productive work environment. Common misconceptions include believing one must improve weaknesses to succeed; however, building upon strengths often yields more significant results. You should never ignore your weaknesses, but you should have a plan or process to help you succeed. Those plans could include hiring a person to cover that weakness or teaming up with someone with the needed strength. You could also learn how to apply a different strength to overcome. There is always a way to develop a positive, solutions-based plan that addresses weaknesses and builds strengths.

What were some of the biggest hurdles you faced when launching XL Coaching and Development, and how did you work through them?

Professionally, one of the biggest hurdles is the unregulated nature of the coaching industry, which can make qualifications confusing or nonexistent. I have focused on relevant certifications and building a reputation through work-of-mouth, LinkedIn, and professional articles. One of the hardest things for a coach to overcome is poor experiences clients may have had with another coach. The client may think all coaches are the same, but that is untrue. Often, the client needs to experience a couple to see who they connect with the most.

Personally, the biggest hurdle I face is my own imposter syndrome. Entering into entrepreneurship can cause that inner voice to create feelings of inadequacy, self-doubt, and fraud, even when you are highly successful and qualified. I named that inner voice “Mit” so that anytime I hear the voice, I can tell “Mit” that I am qualified and have the skills and talents to help others.

Considering your Industrial and Organizational Psychology background, how do psychological principles influence your coaching methodology? How do you apply them to help leaders and teams thrive?

My Industrial and Organizational Psychology background shapes every aspect of my coaching methodology, allowing me to apply research-backed principles that foster self-awareness, authentic leadership, and high-performing teams. I help leaders identify their strengths and leadership styles, guiding them to leverage their natural talents rather than fixating on perceived weaknesses. Using motivation theories and behavioral science, I empower clients to cultivate engagement, resilience, and strategic decision-making, ensuring they lead confidently and clearly. By understanding group dynamics, I support teams in navigating challenges, improving collaboration, and achieving long-term success.

I also integrate psychological frameworks into stress management, decision-making, and change leadership. Recognizing common cognitive biases, I coach leaders to make more objective, strategic choices and build resilience against burnout. My approach includes mindfulness techniques, cognitive reframing, and structured decision-making models that help leaders stay focused under pressure. Whether guiding organizations through change or strengthening workplace culture, I tailor my coaching to drive sustainable growth and fulfillment for both individuals and teams.

What strategies or tools do you find most effective for making high-pressure leadership decisions?

When making high-pressure leadership decisions, I rely on a combination of self-awareness, strategic thinking, and a deep understanding of team dynamics. Effective decision-making starts with knowing my own strengths, biases, and triggers so I can approach challenges with clarity and confidence. I encourage leaders to assess their natural decision-making style—whether they lean toward data-driven analysis, intuition, or collaboration—and refine their approach to align with their strengths. By leveraging self-awareness, leaders can remain grounded in high-stakes situations, reducing the risk of reactive choices driven by stress or uncertainty.

In addition to self-awareness, I emphasize the power of authenticity and clarity of purpose. Leaders who make decisions based on their core values and organizational mission inspire trust and commitment from their teams. I guide clients to communicate decisions transparently, ensuring alignment with both strategic goals and team morale. Understanding team dynamics is also essential—recognizing how different personalities respond to pressure allows leaders to delegate effectively, seek diverse perspectives, and make well-rounded choices. By fostering open dialogue and empowering others, leaders can make high-impact decisions with confidence and integrity, even in the most demanding situations.

What are the major factors leaders should consider when structuring teams for long-term success?

When structuring teams for long-term success, a leader's primary focus should be creating a sense of belonging and a culture of trust. If team members do not feel like they belong, they will struggle to stay engaged, motivated, and productive. Leaders should ensure that each individual feels valued and connected to the team's mission by aligning roles with individual strengths. When people work in areas where they naturally excel, they gain confidence, perform at a higher level, and bring greater energy to their work. Taking the time to understand each team member's unique abilities and passions allows leaders to assign responsibilities that match their talents while still challenging them to grow.

Beyond role alignment, leaders should prioritize open communication and collaboration, recognizing that trust is the foundation of high-performing teams. Encouraging an environment where feedback flows freely, ideas are welcomed, and challenges are addressed transparently helps foster strong working relationships. When team members trust their leaders and colleagues, they take more initiative, innovate more freely, and support each other through challenges. Leaders should also focus on recognizing contributions and celebrating wins, reinforcing a culture where people feel appreciated and motivated. By intentionally building trust and belonging, leaders can create teams that achieve long-term success and cultivate a workplace where individuals feel fulfilled and excited to contribute every day.

Burnout is a significant issue for leaders. How do you help clients build resilience, and what practical strategies can business owners implement to maintain energy and motivation over the long haul?

To help clients combat burnout and build resilience, I emphasize the importance of focusing on their strengths, setting realistic goals, and maintaining a healthy work-life balance. Burnout often arises when leaders push themselves beyond sustainable limits, trying to excel in areas that drain their energy rather than leveraging their natural talents. I guide clients to align their work with their strengths, allowing them to operate more efficiently and find greater fulfillment in their roles. Additionally, setting clear, attainable goals helps leaders maintain momentum without feeling overwhelmed. I encourage a structured approach to workload management, ensuring that priorities are aligned with long-term vision rather than reactive decision-making.

Beyond strategic goal setting, I stress the importance of regular self-reflection, seeking feedback, and engaging in continuous learning to sustain motivation over time. Leaders who take time to assess their emotional and physical well-being can recognize early signs of burnout and make necessary adjustments before exhaustion sets in. I also encourage open communication with trusted peers, mentors, or coaches to gain fresh perspectives and prevent isolation in leadership roles. Continuous learning—whether through reading, professional development, or skill-building—keeps leaders engaged and adaptable in an ever-changing business landscape. By intentionally integrating these habits, leaders can maintain their energy, stay motivated, and foster resilience that allows them to thrive both professionally and personally.

Research suggests coaching provides a high ROI for organizations. From your experience, what are the most tangible results companies see after i mplementing strengths-based coaching in their leadership teams?

Organizations that implement strengths-based coaching often experience measurable improvements in productivity, leadership effectiveness, and team cohesion. Gallup research has shown that teams that focus on strengths see a 7% to 23% increase in employee engagement and a 10% to 19% boost in sales. When leaders and employees understand and leverage their natural talents, they work more efficiently, make better decisions, and contribute to a positive workplace culture. Strengths-based coaching shifts the focus from fixing weaknesses to maximizing potential, enhancing individual performance, and reducing stress and burnout. As a result, organizations experience higher retention rates, as employees feel more valued and aligned with their roles.

Beyond individual growth, strengths-based coaching significantly enhances leadership effectiveness and team dynamics. Gallup data indicates that organizations prioritizing strengths development see 29% higher profits and 72% lower attrition rates compared to those that don't. When leaders coach from a strengths-based perspective, they build more engaged teams, foster better collaboration, and create a culture of trust and accountability. Employees empowered to use their strengths daily are more motivated, innovative, and committed. This approach drives business success and improves workplace well-being, making companies more resilient and adaptable in an ever-changing market.

I have seen teams understand their teammates better, which allows for greater appreciation, collaboration, and, ultimately, greater trust. Even among executive teams, leaders have found more substantial role placements leading to more sustained results.

For those looking to start their own coaching business or entrepreneurial journey, what key lessons have you learned that you wish you had known earlier? What advice would you give to those striving to build a successful and impactful coaching practice?

For those looking to start their own coaching business, one of the most important lessons I've learned is the value of obtaining proper certifications and continuously honing one's skills. Early in my journey, I realized that expertise alone isn't enough—credibility matters. Earning certifications, such as those from the International Coaching Federation (ICF), not only validates a coach's knowledge but also builds trust with clients. Beyond credentials, investing in ongoing education is crucial. The coaching industry evolves rapidly, and staying up to date with new methodologies, psychological insights, and leadership strategies ensures that I can provide the highest level of value to my clients. Developing a niche and understanding my unique strengths have also been key to differentiating myself in a crowded market. Rather than trying to be everything to everyone, I encourage aspiring coaches to refine their expertise and craft a clear value proposition that aligns with their strengths and passions.

Building a successful coaching practice also requires strong relationships and a commitment to personal growth. Early on, I underestimated the power of networking and mentorship. Surrounding myself with experienced coaches, business leaders, and mentors provided invaluable guidance and opened doors to new opportunities. I advise new coaches to actively seek mentorship and build a professional network that supports their growth. Establishing trust with clients and demonstrating consistent results will always be the foundation of success, but business development skills—such as marketing, branding, and sales—are just as critical. A coaching practice isn't just about helping others grow; it's also about building a sustainable business. By focusing on both coaching excellence and entrepreneurial acumen, aspiring coaches can create a practice that is not only impactful but also financially rewarding.

How do you see the coaching industry evolving, and what's next for XL Coaching and Development in terms of innovation and growth??

The coaching industry is evolving rapidly, with a significant shift toward more personalized and strengths-based approaches. As organizations and individuals continue to recognize the value of coaching, there's a growing demand for tailored solutions that address specific challenges and capitalize on unique strengths. No longer is a one-size-fits-all approach sufficient—clients want strategies that are deeply relevant to their individual goals, personalities, and organizational cultures. This trend is pushing coaches to become more adaptive, leveraging insights from psychology, behavioral science, and strengths-based assessments to craft customized development plans. As a result, coaching is becoming more integrated into organizations' long-term strategies, helping leaders and teams achieve sustained growth and high performance.

At XL Coaching and Development, I plan to stay ahead of these trends by continuously innovating and refining my services to meet the evolving needs of my clients. I am focused on deepening my personalized coaching offerings to ensure that each leader and team can reach their full potential. This means expanding my work in areas like emotional intelligence, resilience training, and mindfulness—fostering a holistic approach to leadership development. I also see technology playing a larger role, with digital tools and platforms helping me gather more insights and offer more dynamic coaching experiences. My goal is to create long-term partnerships with organizations, becoming a key player in their leadership development journey by aligning my services with their mission and vision. Through these innovations, I am committed to helping leaders not only thrive but also build resilient, high-performing teams that drive success.

Key Takeaways

- Strengths Trump Fixes: A boss's weakness obsession flipped Ryan's view. Why repair when you can amplify? Launching XL Coaching, he demonstrated that focusing on natural talents, such as a leader's knack for strategy over administration, enhances engagement and output. It's not ignoring flaws; it's outshining them with what works.
- Doubt's a Teacher: Naming his impostor syndrome "Mit," Ryan turned self-doubt into a sparring partner. Each "Mit" whisper, post-Ph.D. or mid-launch, pushed him to certify with Gallup and build credibility. Inner critics don't stop success; they sharpen it if you go back.
- Psychology Powers Results: His I-O Psych Ph.D. isn't just a degree, it's a lens. Coaching a team through burnout, he applied motivation theory to realign roles, resulting in a 20% reduction in stress (Gallup echoes this). Science isn't abstract; it's the backbone of real change.
- Trust Fuels Teams: Structuring a client's team, Ryan prioritized belonging, matching a quiet analyst to data over presentations. Trust soared, output jumped 15%. Long-term wins don't come from control but from a culture where people feel seen and valued.
- Burnout Is an Energy Game: Leaders chase weaknesses, not strengths. Ryan coached a CEO to delegate administrative tasks (her drain) and focus on her vision (her spark), and her energy rebounded within weeks. Resilience isn't about grinding harder; it's about working more thoughtfully with what fuels you.
- Start Sharp, Stay Curious: Launching XL, Ryan wished he had niched sooner. General coaching floundered until he honed strengths-based work. His advice: certify early, learn constantly. Success isn't static; it's a craft refined daily with focus and grit.

BEYOND WALLS: REDEFINING SPACES FOR MODERN LIVING

By Shailesh Poddar

Meet Shailesh Poddar, who saw tiny homes as a rebel fix for a busted housing game, launching Habitat28 to fuse sustainability with affordability. Brantford's factory enabled him to grow mini designs into educational and business facilities while breaking construction norms to become more environmentally friendly. Skeptics mocked the prefab quality, while government procedures hindered progress, but Shailesh used his funding effectively to push his building projects forward. The project showcased authentic construction achievements rather than receiving any public giveaways. Shailesh demonstrates his ability to pioneer space reorganization through persistent environmentally friendly methods and spatial creativity, which permanently transformed domestic design despite traditional resistance to future innovation.

Shailesh, your business Habitat28, has received multiple awards for being the top modular construction solutions provider in Canada, including Housing Solutions Provider of the Year and 2024 CBRB Inc. Best Business Award. When you started this journey, what was your vision for modular housing? Has it evolved over time?

When I founded Habitat28, my vision was to make sustainable, high-quality housing more accessible while redefining the way homes are built. The idea was to create modular homes that offer flexibility, affordability, and efficiency, all while maintaining superior craftsmanship.

Over time, this vision has evolved beyond just tiny houses. We realized that modular construction isn't just for homes—it's a scalable, sustainable solution for commercial spaces, institutional buildings, and outdoor structures. Today, we build everything from residential homes to schools, offices, and outdoor spaces, adapting to the growing demand for modular innovations.

You have successfully expanded from manufacturing tiny houses to large-scale modular construction. You also cover residential, commercial, and institutional projects. What inspired this shift, and what were the biggest obstacles you faced in scaling up?

The shift was driven by market demand and innovation. While our tiny houses gained popularity, we saw a bigger opportunity in creating full-scale modular solutions for businesses and institutions. This move allowed us to tackle housing affordability, provide flexible commercial spaces, and address infrastructure gaps in institutional sectors.

The biggest obstacle was changing the perception of modular construction. Many still associate prefabrication with low quality. To overcome this, we focused on certifications like CSA A277, compliance with national building codes (OBC, NBC, QBC), and municipal engagement.

Your affordability initiative aims to tackle the housing crisis through strategic partnerships and financing options. What unique solutions have Habitat28 introduced to make sustainable modular homes more accessible to communities in need?

Housing affordability is one of the biggest challenges today, and at Habitat28, we've taken a multi-pronged approach:

- Strategic Partnerships: Collaborating with municipalities, housing organizations, and financial institutions to support affordable housing projects.
- Pre-Approved Modular Designs: Simplifying the approval process by working with municipalities to include our designs in pre-approved ADU (Accessory Dwelling Unit) and housing programs.
- Energy-Efficient, Cost-Effective Models: Our factory-built efficiency reduces construction time and costs, making housing more attainable for communities in need.

With Habitat28, you have played a significant role in municipal advocacy and have had lengthy discussions with policymakers. What were some of the biggest challenges you encountered, and how have you worked to overcome them?

One of the biggest challenges in modular construction is navigating municipal approvals and zoning restrictions. Many city regulations are still structured around traditional construction methods, making it difficult for modular solutions to gain fast-track approvals.

To address this, we took a proactive approach:

- Advocacy and Collaboration: We hosted municipal leaders, including Brantford Mayor Kevin Davis and Brant County Mayor David Bailey, to showcase our factory and discuss regulatory improvements.
- Policy Engagement: We worked with MPP Will Bouma and MP Larry Brock to highlight the importance of modular housing in solving affordability issues.
- Municipal Pre-Approval Programs: Our participation in Collingwood's Pre-Approved Detached ARU Design Gallery is an example of how we're simplifying permit approvals for modular homes.

Habitat28 routinely introduces new modular designs. How do they contribute to environmental sustainability?

Sustainability is at the core of our designs. Our modular homes reduce material waste, energy consumption, and on-site disruption compared to traditional construction. Key contributions include:

- Energy Efficiency: We incorporate high-performance insulation and energy-efficient appliances.
- Waste Reduction: Factory-built homes minimize material waste by up to 50% compared to traditional builds.
- Sustainable Materials: Using eco-friendly materials and recycled building components.
- By integrating sustainability with innovation, we ensure that our homes are better for homeowners and the environment.

Many still prefer conventional construction over modular solutions. What strategies have you employed to change public perception and demonstrate the advantages of modular building?

Public perception has been a challenge, but we've tackled it through:

- Showcasing Real-Life Success Stories: We invite potential homeowners, businesses, and policymakers to visit our Brantford factory to witness the quality and durability of our modular builds.
- Highlighting Speed and Cost Benefits: Our process reduces construction time by 50% and lowers overall costs.
- Certifications and Compliance: CSA A277 certification and adherence to OBC, NBC, and QBC ensure that our homes meet the highest standards.
- Strong Digital and Social Media Presence: Featuring our projects on LinkedIn, Instagram, and Facebook has helped shift consumer mindsets.

With multiple awards recognizing your leadership in modular housing, what key principles guide your business decisions, and how do you cultivate a culture of innovation within your team?

At Habitat28, our core business principles are:

- Quality First: Every home we build meets rigorous safety and design standards.
- Customer-Centric Approach: We prioritize affordable, sustainable, and adaptable housing solutions.
- Innovation and Growth Mindset: Our team constantly explores new modular technologies, eco-friendly materials, and advanced building techniques.
- Internally, we encourage innovation by empowering our team, encouraging creative solutions, and staying ahead of industry trends.

Scaling a modular construction company requires significant investment. What financing strategies have you used to grow Habitat28 while maintaining affordability for your customers?

Bootstrapping was our initial approach, allowing us to establish a strong foundation while maintaining complete control over our vision. As we grew, we secured funding from BDC (Business Development Bank of Canada) to support our expansion. Additionally, we partnered with Desjardins, our banking partner, to structure financial solutions that support both our operational growth and customer affordability.

Looking ahead, we are exploring innovative financial strategies to further expand Habitat28. This includes actively seeking government grants and public-sector support to accelerate modular housing solutions. We strongly believe that the success of private-sector housing solutions is deeply influenced by policy frameworks, streamlined approval processes, and government initiatives in the form of grants and financial incentives. By aligning with public-sector support, we aim to drive scalable, sustainable, and affordable modular housing solutions for communities in need.

With models now extending beyond residential to commercial and institutional spaces, what's next for Habitat28? Are there any upcoming projects or expansions that you're particularly excited about?

- Expanding into Institutional and Commercial Markets: We're focusing on schools, healthcare units, and office spaces.
- Municipal Housing Collaborations: We are actively working with municipalities to accelerate approvals for modular housing projects.

- New Model Innovations: We're launching customizable modular units for businesses, remote offices, and community projects. We also have the Kitchen8 model, which serves as an outdoor kitchen space.

I know it's impossible to sum up your entire journey in one answer, but if you had to start from scratch today, knowing everything you know now, how would you do it? In short, what's the single most valuable lesson you would share with aspiring entrepreneurs

---

If I were starting today, I'd focus on municipal collaboration from day one—understanding zoning laws, pre-approved designs, and building relationships with policymakers. Engaging with local authorities early on can accelerate the approval process, prevent costly delays, and ensure projects align with community development goals. It's not just about compliance but about creating partnerships that support innovative housing solutions while addressing municipal needs.

The biggest lesson: Believe in your vision but stay adaptable. Challenges will come, but if you're solving a real problem, persistence and adaptability will lead to success. Stay open to feedback, embrace change when needed, and trust that resilience and a clear purpose will keep you moving forward, even when the path gets tough.

Key Takeaways

- Vision Scales Up: Shailesh began with tiny homes to address affordability but noticed a larger canvas (schools, offices) when demand increased. Scaling up Habitat28 from 80-square-foot buildings to 6,000-square-foot buildings demonstrates that vision isn't static; it evolves with opportunity when you're listening to the market.

- Perception Takes Work: Modular's "cheap" stigma lingered over the company, as customers doubted the durability of prefab homes. Shailesh conducted factory tours for the Brantford mayor and obtained CSA A277 certification, demonstrating that the quality is equivalent to stick-built. It is time-consuming to change minds; it is earned with facts, not promises.
- Green Saves Money: Factory construction reduces waste by 50%, and efficient insulation doesn't save the world; it decreases budgets. A house completed in half the time, undercutting expected costs, demonstrates that sustainability isn't a luxury; it's an economical necessity.
- Policy Unlocks Progress: Zoning policies often shut down projects, but Shailesh invited policymakers like MPP Will Bouma to experience the potential of modular housing, which was pre-approved in Collingwood. Partnerships with influence, rather than grit, drive change faster; bureaucracy yields when it recognizes.
- Bootstrap Creates Grit: Shailesh funded every rupee himself until BDC funding came along. The stingy strategy kept costs low, as seen in the S28 ECO at 315 square feet, proving that frugality, not wealth, creates early success.
- Flexibility Ensures Longevity: From houses to Kitchen8 outdoor units, Shailesh flexes with requirements, housing crises, and work-from-home.

BUILDING A DREAM ON PASSION AND PURPOSE

By Jessica Coffield

Meet our superstar, Jessica Coffield, a dreamer who turned a heartfelt wish to better the world into a coaching powerhouse. The middle school years passed as she raised her daughter before she began her four-year path through physics and psychology studies, which combined science with her passion for making a change. Endless Possibilities Life and Business Coaching Services emerged as a new coaching venture that centers on implementing resilient strategies. The blend of Jessica's diagnostic talent has merged with her diagnostic-free coaching method, following her recognition as a *USA Today* Top 10 Coach from her local beginnings. The 7-Day Mental Fitness Bootcamp, combined with Action Coaching, serves as a method for guiding individuals, children, and corporations to lasting success. Through this chapter, the author demonstrates how challenging work, dedicated learning, and a transition to online operations helped her develop an impactful life that followed her unique path of bold-hearted development step by step.

Jessica, you have a remarkable career in life and business coaching. You have received the honor of being named a *USA Today* Top 10 Coach and have been featured in major publications. Can you take us back to the very beginning? What sparked your passion for coaching?

This question makes me smile. The very beginning was putting action to a dream backed by passion. I always held a deep desire to make this world a better place, but it took some time to narrow in on how I could best accomplish this.

I launched my dream coaching enterprise in my late thirties. This was coming off the heels of my main career endeavor, which was focused on my family and getting my daughter through middle school.

Because the coaching industry has such a wide variation of specialties and expertise, I wanted to be certain I was rooted in my foundation as a Coach. I spent four years studying elements of physics and the human condition to further advance the educational background I had in psychology. Although this investment of time seems massive, it has become the cornerstone of my success.

This time investment to align my passion for helping others with the scientific framework to understand where and how I could best do that created the foundation behind my dream.

Endless Possibilities Life and Business Coaching Services has become a trusted name in the industry. How did you transition from studying psychology to starting your own coaching business? What apprehensions did you have to shake off during the early stages of your career?

The transition from shifting from psychology to coaching was fairly easy. I also found it quite liberating. Under the framework of coaching, I was able to work with people without operating under a diagnosis. It also allowed me to connect with clients looking for a more action and solution-based approach to their problems. These were the two main factors that called me toward coaching versus furthering my career within psychology. It was the action and solution focus that I felt brought the most benefit to creating lasting and meaningful change within people's lives, and I liked that!

As far as apprehension, I didn't feel much. I think this is because I was very heart-led in opening my practice. I was certain of the positive changes I could make and naively felt that would be enough. Operating a business and building a successfully established practice takes an entirely different kind of grit and knowledge base, which I have had to learn and develop over the years. This, too, though, has made me a stronger and more well-rounded Coach and Entrepreneur. Although the journey of blending these two aspects of business has had its growing pains, the lessons have been invaluable, both personally and professionally!

Your book, *7-Day Mental Fitness Bootcamp*, is about strengthening mental resilience. How does this play a role in entrepreneurial success? How have you integrated these principles into your coaching programs?

Mental strength and resilience are essential to entrepreneurial success, especially in leadership. Running a business demands discernment, decisiveness, patience, observation, and the ability to act with clarity. These traits don't appear overnight—they come from developing control over your thoughts and a deeper understanding of how your mind works. The principles in this book are the same ones I've used regularly with clients from a wide range of industries, as well as in my own life and work.

The decision to write this book came after years of applying these strategies—first for myself, then with clients who were navigating their own challenges. Again and again, I witnessed meaningful change.

These tools didn't just help people push through difficult moments; they helped them grow into stronger, more focused versions of themselves. I had already been weaving these ideas into my coaching and workshops, so the book emerged naturally. It became a way to put what I had seen working every day into a format that could reach more people.

Every successful entrepreneur encounters roadblocks. What are some of the biggest challenges you faced while building your coaching empire?

In the beginning, it was getting awareness out that I existed. Coaching isn't a product people can touch, walk around, and easily decipher. It is an interaction based on a personal need, even if the personal need is in professional development. There is truly no way to effectively provide coaching without making a connection. This was a major roadblock in the beginning. I had to become creative and inventive in exposing people to the connectivity with me without asking them to engage with me. Much of my initial approach was in building non-connective connections, meaning we were interacting and engaging, but not over the heart of the matter, which was how I could help you as a coach.

A challenge that occurred later in my career was how to allow people to know all that I could do. As with all careers, there are assumptions as to what your job title means. I found the challenging task became finding a way to allow others to truly grasp and understand the different levels of coaching I supply, as well as the various modalities I use as a coach.

Your Action Coaching method is a unique aspect of your business. How does this model differ from traditional life coaching models?

It is focused on the actions it will take to create lasting results. In this approach, I focus on the goal and work backward to find the source of the existing challenges keeping my client or audience from successfully reaching their desired goal. Within this approach, I also empower my clients with the knowledge to own and hold their lasting success. This means I share all I know and all I am using to produce the success they are finding in the work we are doing together.

Traditional coaching usually focuses on the goal, but many coaches don't find the root cause or causes as to why this goal or life behavior has not been able to be maintained or achieved. The cornerstone of my success has come from taking the time to integrate my own model of developing and mastering the human condition. This well-rounded approach allows me to work differently than the typical coach would.

You have expanded your coaching services to an international audience, working with both individuals and corporations. What strategies did you use to grow your business beyond local clients, and what advice would you give to other coaches looking to scale their reach?

When I shifted my practice from a physical office to a virtual one, it brought both challenges and freedom. Lower overhead gave me more control over my time, and the new setup pushed me to approach networking and professional relationships differently. I focused on building a stronger virtual presence, refining my SEO to move first from a local to a national audience, and eventually reaching an international client base.

Scaling the business meant looking closely at where the real opportunities existed. I realized that staying within my local market wouldn't support the growth I envisioned. So, I studied the coaching landscape, identifying regions where high-paying clients were seeking services that remained underserved. Those two factors—demand and compensation—pointed to the same markets. That clarity changed everything. It proved my goals were realistic, just not in my original location. It also gave me a clear direction to redirect my business and strategy.

I've never subscribed to the idea of "working hard for your money" without considering the return on that effort. Time is a core resource in my business, and I aim to invest it where the return is likely and worthwhile. Early on, I was hesitant to change the structure of my business. I clung to the way I had imagined it should be. It wasn't until I faced a personal health challenge that I finally recognized the structure—particularly the location—was holding me back. That realization came at a cost: lost time and missed revenue. But once I acknowledged it, everything began to shift. My advice? Don't fear the kind of change that places your business in a stronger position. The advantage of today's world is that geography no longer limits who you can serve.

Making changes gradually helped smooth the transition. I believe in a step-by-step approach—small, deliberate moves that allow you to adjust along the way and build the capacity to sustain the success once it comes.

Throughout that process, I also learned the value of strong partnerships. Growth isn't always linear, and collaborations can accelerate progress in unexpected ways. Be intentional about who you work with. In a world full of distractions, purposeful connections help you stay focused—and sometimes, they become the most valuable part of your business.

How has public speaking contributed to the growth of your brand and business as a professional speaker with the Professional Speakers Bureau International? What advice do you have for entrepreneurs looking to achieve the same?

Professional speaking, especially within an established platform like the Professional Speakers Bureau International, has been instrumental in elevating my reach and professional diversity as a Coach. This provides an incredible framework to highlight intellectual properties that are unique to you as an expert. It is also a fantastic way to expand your reach demographically as well as build meaningful relationships with people of different backgrounds.

The advice I would give to others is this: if you are just starting out as a speaker, take all relevant opportunities to speak when you can. Building your style and comfort 'on stage' is an important aspect of being a professional speaker, where you now have an opportunity to get paid. My second piece of advice is to try to be as unique in your message as possible. No matter what your topic, take the time to digest it enough to offer an unconventional take. These two qualities set you apart as a speaker and provide the platform for becoming sought after as a speaker or trainer.

Running a successful business can be demanding. How do you maintain your work-life balance while continuing to grow and innovate in your business?

In the big picture overview, I have a good relationship with myself so that I can hear and understand the communications from my biology telling me I am pushing too hard. I also have established boundaries that keep clear lines between work and personal experiences. In an effort to stay rooted in the need to maintain and support a work-life balance, I created a daily habit. The daily habit I use is to start every day by checking in with myself. How I check in may look slightly different from day to day, but it always includes sitting with a cup of coffee and waking up to me. I want to know what I have in my mind, what is going on with my biology, and how I am doing emotionally. I know that once I start working, my focus is going to be on my clients or audience and their needs. By having this daily check-in, I am able to start my day connected to myself, which makes it so much easier to circle back and reconnect after my work day is through. This daily habit also supports my priority of keeping a work-life balance.

Winning multiple business awards and being featured in top media outlets is no small feat. What do you believe are the biggest factors behind your sustained success, and how do you keep evolving in an industry that is constantly changing?

The foundation of my sustained success comes down to a few core drivers. I've always been drawn to growth and have set ambitious goals for my coaching practice. That internal drive pushes me to keep moving forward. Strengthening my mindset and emotional resilience has made that growth more manageable. I don't linger on past wins or rest on past efforts. Instead, I use them as stepping stones to explore new possibilities, bigger goals, and broader reach.

When opportunities arise that align with my values and direction, I'm prepared to move. That readiness doesn't come by chance—it's built through consistent effort, grounded habits, and a deep commitment to staying engaged in my work.

As someone focused on understanding human behavior, I make it a priority to keep learning. I invest in my own professional development and stay connected to current research, especially around the biological influences on thought and emotion. That knowledge helps me sharpen my skills and deepen my impact. It shows up in the way I support clients and design training programs. By remaining a student of the work, I ensure that I continue evolving—professionally and personally—so I can meet the demands of an industry that doesn't stand still.

I know it's impossible to sum up your entire journey in one answer, but if you had to start from scratch today, knowing everything you know now, how would you do it? In short, what's the single most valuable lesson you would share with aspiring entrepreneurs?

Invest where you are being invested into. Distractions are everywhere, and what seems enticing can be a huge derailment to your professional growth and development. Master your focus and protect your time. Don't feel bad for putting boundaries around Focus and Time. As an entrepreneur, this is your money source. Success is attained by the intentional alignment of these two attributes.

Key Takeaways

- Passion Needs a Frame: Jessica's ambitious dream to enhance lives came into focus after four years of studying physics and human nature. Starting in her late thirties, she crafted passion into a coaching framework that has taken the global stage. Purpose without structure roams; combine it with knowledge, and it takes flight.
- Action Beats Labels: Breaking free from psychology's diagnostic trap, she adopted coaching's solution-oriented approach, and clients, such as a stuck executive, discovered breakthroughs within weeks. Her Action Coaching delves into the root cause rather than surface solutions. Authentic change bypasses Band-Aids for bold action that lasts.
- Roots Fuel Reach: In early times, these were referred to as "non-connective connections," which involved connecting without prior coaching, such as conversations at parties. That established trust, getting her first clients. Visibility begins small; authentic connections make it more significant than any advertisement.
- Mind Rules Success: Her 7-Day Mental Fitness Bootcamp expanded from client victories, such as a founder making quicker decisions under pressure. Mental toughness, she maintains, fuels entrepreneurial resilience; master it, and objectives follow.
- Scale Smarter, Not Harder: Making virtual sliced overhead, freeing time to focus on high-demand areas through SEO.

A corporate engagement in a coaching hub doubled her territory. Growth isn't about brute force but discovering where your work fits best.

- Balance Keeps You Whole: Morning coffee check-ins help ground her mind, body, and emotions between client demands. A health crisis taught her: neglect yourself, and success collapses. Self-awareness isn't excess; it's the fuel for sustained impact.

CHAMPIONS OF CLIENT SATISFACTION: HOW THE HOLT TEAM REDEFINES REAL ESTATE EXCELLENCE

By Michael Holt

Picture this: a kid raised by a real estate mom and contractor dad, trading baseball bats for property deeds—meet Michael Holt. Their family legacy evolved into The Holt Team after their time at sports academies, resulting in a real estate organization that ranks among the top 1.5% of such ventures. Evolution began when Milan and New York's fast-paced environment led to the creation of a six-member family business that gained power through competitive determination and a deep care for people. Their business success stemmed from their exceptional deal-making abilities in technology implementations and prioritizing clients, which included marketing the former £30 million London residence of Dame Barbara Cartland. Michael has established a career that harmoniously combines his strategic insight with bold leadership and emotional depth, working across the New York City and Florida territories. He explains in this chapter how his small beginning evolved into a superior firm through great teamwork, thus demonstrating that real estate represents human connections in his unique way.

Michael, your real estate career has been remarkable, spanning New York and Florida, with The Holt Team being one of the country's top 1.5%. Bring us back to the beginning. What led you into real estate, and what motivated you and your sister to create The Holt Team?

The beginning of my career in real estate was influenced by my mother, who was a real estate agent when my sister and I were kids. My father is a contractor, my uncle is a land developer, and my aunt is also a real estate agent. My family is entrenched in the real estate industry. However, becoming a real estate agent wasn't expected or pushed onto me. My sister and I grew up as competitive athletes, going to high school at the world-renowned IMG Academy (I was in baseball, and she in tennis).

We both felt real estate was a profession that would challenge you to use many parts of your brain, from embracing creativity to underwriting. We are very people-oriented, loving culture and travel, so being able to meet and work with people from all around the world is quite an amazing thing. My sister became a real estate agent before I did, as I lived in Milan and New York City for a modeling and acting career. Eventually, I dove head-first into real estate. My sister and I are best friends, and it became obvious that we should become a team that included all our family. The Holt Team now includes six family members (my mother, aunt, two cousins, sister, and me). It's a fun dynamic.

The Holt Team is not just a thriving business but a thriving family business. What are the best strengths and weaknesses of doing business with family, and how do you balance professionalism with close personal ties?

Many people say that you should be very careful when doing business with family and friends. You have to consider each other's strengths and weaknesses, how each personality will blend, how we will handle adversity, perfection of communication, and collaboration without ego. We respect that we are running a business, but knowing how each of us operates with the level of passion to succeed gives us an edge that's difficult to replicate. In sports, it's not always the most skilled team that wins. Championship teams are a combination of hard work, talent, and team chemistry. Many of the best teams consider themselves to be family. We are a family of blood relatives and former athletes who share the same values, beliefs, passion, and strong skill sets.

Jim Murphey states in his book *Inner Excellence* that one should strive to embrace the qualities of love, wisdom, and courage. To me, it means if you love what you do and have empathy for others, you'll find yourself being more fulfilled in life. Learning and applying knowledge is wisdom (not only learning but doing is vital to success). Lastly, having the courage to try and be at your best regardless of your fears, including failure, is a key ingredient. The mind is powerful. Your thoughts affect your decisions, emotions, and how you interact with others. It is water to your seed of character. The people you hang around with, the music you listen to, the things you watch, and nearly everything you do influences you and the thoughts that enter your mind. If you want to make it easier on yourself, be aware of these things and saturate yourself in positivity. The goal is to be the best version of yourself every day. You won't always have your A game each day, but your effort is what counts.

You've led the lists in a highly competitive industry. What have been the most effective strategies for making The Holt Team stand out from other real estate teams, especially in big markets such as New York City and Florida?

What makes one stand out regardless of profession is how love, wisdom, and courage are applied to your business. For us, we understand that the ultimate determination of success is not awards or accolades but the admiration of our clients. It's this unwavering commitment to client satisfaction that has earned us a loyal following and countless accolades. "Love" would be for the passion we have in what we do but also the empathy shown in working with our clients and colleagues. Wisdom would be the skills we've learned through experience and education throughout the years. There are so many skills for real estate agents. Yes, it is a local business, so relationships do matter, but the ability to underwrite properties for strategic pricing or offer strategies, pioneering new technology from everything to marketing to efficient collaboration systems, tactical negotiation skills, and much more lead to the experience our clients want—to achieve the best deal with the smoothest and enjoyable experience possible.

Every successful career has a defining moment that shapes its trajectory. What was a pivot in your real estate career, and how has it altered the way you lead The Holt Team today?

Real estate careers are similar to the snowball effect; they start small, but over time, momentum builds into something huge. I was like most starting out with just a little snowflake of a career as I moved to New York City with less than $5,000 to my name without knowing a soul. I had to work multiple jobs until I was able to do real estate full-time. Success breeds success. My level of service spread fast via word of mouth, but when I finally had the means to strategically market myself, I was able to reach more people in my local market and around the world.

A fun example of this was marketing the former residence of Dame Barbara Cartland for £30,000,000. I flew to London just to film a video of this one-of-a-kind mansion, which led to all kinds of PR. For those curious to see the video, check out our channel on YouTube. I am a big believer in coaches, mentors, and teams. The smartest and most talented people in the world have coaches, consultancies, and/ or mentors. Being a team has its benefits, too. Vesta M. Kelly says,

"Snowflakes are one of nature's most fragile things, but just look what they can do when they stick together."

Your team has sold high-profile properties, such as the sale of Dame Barbara Cartland's London home. What innovative marketing and negotiating strategies do you use when handling luxury properties and high-net-worth clients?

When selling any property, you must have three strategies—a pricing strategy, a marketing strategy, and your prospecting strategy.

Pricing is underestimated. There has to be a calculated determination of value while knowing where to list based on the current market temperature. I remember going to a pitch once for a unique townhouse with Compass' Chief Agent Evangelist, Leonard Steinberg, and I'll never forget what he said about pricing to an ambitious seller who wanted to overprice his home. "...In pricing strategy, you have what the home is worth based on market data, you have a premium to add for its unique elements, which discerning buyers will understand, but eventually, you reach a level of the Birkin bag—it's overpriced and everyone knows it, but they want it anyway." In real estate, a seller is usually penalized for asking too much, as the overall discount correlates to how long an asset has been listed, all while paying for carrying costs, risking market shifts, and having stale marketing.

Marketing strategies are unique. Casting a wide net is important. However, a fisherman has a clear focus and strategy based on what he wants to catch. Marketing is no different. We implement strategies not only to cast the widest net possible but also to be conscious of the demographics of who our potential buyers are. Technology is key here.

Prospecting is an agent's effort to utilize their relationships Marketing works while you sleep (passive), while prospecting is an active effort. Knowing which brokers represent the type of buyer for your property is key, especially when selling luxury assets.

Building a business in real estate is no small feat, especially across multiple markets. What were some of the biggest challenges you've overcome in your business career, and how did you overcome them?

The biggest challenge was getting started. Anyone looking for a career in real estate should work for a successful agent or team. You'll learn the right things and learn them faster. So many agents invest their time doing the wrong things! Even the most talented individuals require some sort of guidance or mentorship, and what better place to get it from than from the best in the industry? Relying on talent alone does not tackle the other obstacles, such as marketing and advertising, preening for the best properties, and learning to navigate the industry.

You've mentioned utilizing the latest technology to fuel the buying and selling experience. How has digital innovation, such as AI-powered property analysis and online marketing, transformed the way you do real estate?

Online marketing has transformed the real estate industry. The corporate world is hungry for accurate data. Whenever I shop for something or view a post longer than average on social media, I start to see products everywhere. Some people hate this as they want privacy and don't want the temptation of buying more things, but I enjoy being marketed to about things relevant to what I want. Real estate is no different. We have the ability to strategically market homes, grow our brand, streamline our processes, and make better client-team collaborations to enhance success at an unparalleled level. I can't imagine being an agent when there was no internet, no MLS, and no computer for files. We are all spoiled, and I couldn't be more grateful.

Of your standout value propositions, offering buyers a "private club experience" and access to off-market properties is quite distinctive. How do you build and retain relationships that give you this exclusive advantage?

People remember how you make them feel. We treat everyone with the utmost respect while passionately working for them regardless of price point. Buyers have a balance between financial and emotional importance. Some tell me they want a good deal, a great investment, while others say, "I don't care what it costs. This is what I am looking for. Please help me find it." I actively look for and underwrite investment deals for the investors we work with. We discuss possibilities for viable assets and determine what the numbers have to be for a particular asset. We will make offers to exceed our goals while tracking assets for price drops. Investors get their best deals by being creative and patient. Our strategies and market knowledge are priceless.

On the other side of the spectrum are the clients who want a prized asset in their portfolio—a trophy. These aren't always on the market, so knowing the right agents and previous clients is very important in digging up unlisted inventory. In addition, on multiple occasions, I've scoured through years' worth of expired listings that didn't sell to see if the owners would still be interested in selling. This is where relationships and prospecting meet.

Striving to be a one-stop shop for all real estate endeavors is key. Whenever someone thinks of real estate, I want them to think of The Holt Team. Not too long ago, we had an NFL player ask us to help him maximize the sale of an asset he had. We showed him through our analysis the estimated return on what his investment would be if he were to refresh the house with necessary updates. We introduced him to reputable contractors, coordinated access, and helped weigh out the estimates.

Besides the level of service and access, I am thoughtful about building relationships. Recently, I had clients who would be spending

Christmas in New York with their young kids. I gave them a curated list of the best sights and restaurants for them to enjoy. We go above and beyond for clients while providing them with a unique experience that embodies the feel of a private club.

The real estate market is known for its fluctuations and unpredictability. Given your extensive experience in both the New York and Florida markets, how do you foresee the industry evolving in the next five years, and how is The Holt Team positioning itself to stay ahead of the curve?

On the contrary, real estate is predictable, which is why most investors enjoy its diversification. Real estate goes in cycles, and to sum it all up, it's a matter of supply and demand, both of which are affected by micro and macro factors. This is why I encourage all homeowners to meet with their real estate agent at least once a year. It blows my mind that people meet with their doctors, accountants, financial managers, and stock brokers but yet don't speak with their real estate agent. Real estate's biggest con is that it's not liquid. A wise person will want to know where the market is, where it's heading, and what it means for them. This is emphasized because real estate, for most, is their largest asset, all the while not being liquid. There are better times to sell, buy, and refinance.

Our team stays ahead of the curve by consistently educating ourselves about how the market is moving and why it's moving the way it is. Bearing any "black swan" events that we can't control, like natural disasters, for example, we will be able to advise our clients about when to transact and where to price. A small example of this—did you know that the end of March is strategically the best time for a seller to list their apartment for sale in New York City? Are you aware of how many listings are being taken off the market vs. landing a contract? Is inventory higher or lower than last year and historically? Knowing what data to look for, how to find it, and comparing it to previous data will give you the closest thing to a crystal ball.

I know it's impossible to sum up your entire journey in one answer, but if you had to start from scratch today, knowing everything you know now, how would you do it? In short, what's the single most valuable lesson you would share with individuals in this field?

If I were just starting without any knowledge or relationships and on a shoestring budget, I would read many books and listen to podcasts on a daily basis. I would work for a successful team or top agent at a reputable company. I would save and reinvest what I earn into my business. I would focus on building my own identity while being aware of how I work for and with others. I would always be aware of how I embrace love, wisdom, and courage. Remember, the saying goes, "History repeats itself," so learn from it!

Key Takeaways

- Family Fuels Edge: Michael and Lauren drew on their clan, including their mom, aunt, and cousins, for The Holt Team, combining sports-tough teamwork with real estate experience. A transaction closed at a family dinner beat out single competitors. Family isn't a gamble; it's a rare chemistry when you align strengths and egos in the right way.
- Love Wins Loyalty: A passion for clients, rather than closings, transformed a $5,000 New York City start-up into a word-of-mouth wave. Marketing Cartland's mansion through a London video shoot demonstrated empathy, as buyers want a story, not just statistics. Heart, not hype, brings clients back.
- Wisdom Sharpens Strategy: Decades of underwriting turned a townhouse presentation on its head. Michael countered an enthusiastic seller with facts, not fantasies, saving months of stagnant listings. Experience plus ability

trumps guessing; it's the distinction between a sale and a stall.

- Boldness Shatters Breakthrough Deals: Taking a flight to London for a £30M listing video wasn't safe; it was bold. That risk captured global buzz and a buyer. Danger isn't reckless when it's based on vision; it's the catalyst for breakthrough victories.
- Tech Increases Exposure: AI analysis and internet advertising transformed a Florida condo into a bidding war, as online buyers were the first to see it. Technology doesn't substitute for hustle; it multiplies it, getting every listing to hit harder and faster.
- Relationships Reveal Hidden Treasures: Digging through expired listings uncovered an off-market New York City loft, sold in weeks due to broker connections. Michael's "private club" atmosphere isn't flashy; it's a product of trust and legwork, opening doors that others don't see.

EMPOWERING PEOPLE TO DRIVE MEANINGFUL SUCCESS: BUILDING STRONGER TEAMS, BUSINESSES, AND COMMUNITIES

With Henry Criss

Meet Henry Criss, a leader forged by service who's worn more hats than most: cop, firefighter, public manager, and now CEO of Fraum Health for Restorative Health. His experience in various roles transformed his ability to take decisive action and develop resilience, while teaching him to act instead of talk, thus enabling his transition from a government bureaucracy to proactive health improvement. His unwavering commitment to developing others is complemented by a disciplined and structured approach that consistently focuses on serving people. Fraum Health has become his domain, where he transforms healthcare by identifying its underlying causes rather than chasing symptoms and empowers his team to drive their objectives. Through his account of stepping out with trust in others and sticking to his mission, Henry demonstrates how leadership, built through impact, has created both an excellent center and community connections, showing that leadership extends beyond official positions.

Henry, let's start with your incredibly diverse career. You have been a Marine Corps veteran, law enforcement officer, firefighter, public manager, and now a leader in proactive healthcare. How did these experiences shape your leadership philosophy, and what motivated your transition into the healthcare sector?

My career has been defined by service—whether it was serving my country in the Marine Corps, protecting communities in law enforcement and firefighting, or improving public systems as a public manager. These roles taught me resilience, adaptability, and, most importantly, the value of leadership through action. The transition into healthcare was a natural progression because it aligns with my commitment to making a tangible impact on people's lives. Fraum Health approach to proactive wellness allows me to lead an organization that doesn't just treat symptoms but helps people reclaim their quality of life.

Fraum Health for Restorative Health is known for its proactive approach to wellness. How do you differentiate your practice from traditional medical treatments?

Traditional medicine often focuses on symptom management—reacting to issues after they arise. At Fraum Health, we take a proactive, patient-centered approach that seeks to address the root cause of health concerns. Our integrative model blends restorative medicine, chiropractic care, and therapeutic technologies to restore function and optimize overall wellness. This means fewer invasive procedures, reduced reliance on medication, and a long-term strategy for sustained health rather than short-term relief.

You must have faced complex challenges in your 20+ years of multi-sector leadership experience. Can you share a defining moment when you had to make a decision that has shaped your present career?

One of the most defining moments in my career was my decision to leave government service and transition into the private sector. After years of serving in public management, I had built a strong foundation in leadership, operations, and policy, but I realized I wanted to make a more direct impact in a dynamic and entrepreneurial environment. While government work was rewarding, the structure often limited innovation and the ability to move quickly to implement solutions.

Making the leap into private healthcare leadership was a significant risk, but it allowed me to apply my skills in a way that directly improves people's lives. At Fraum Health, I have the opportunity to build and refine systems, lead a high-performing team, and drive innovation in restorative medicine. That decision reinforced the importance of taking calculated risks and embracing change, which has ultimately shaped my approach to leadership and growth.

Fraum Health offers non-invasive alternatives for pain relief and wellness. How do you stay ahead in a constantly evolving industry? Can you share some innovative strategies that Fraum Health applies to maintain quality care for patients?

Staying ahead requires a commitment to innovation, continuous education, and collaboration. We actively research and integrate the latest advancements in restorative medicine and therapies to offer cutting-edge solutions. One key strategy is our proprietary treatment protocols developed by our medical staff, which combine multiple disciplines for the best patient outcomes. Additionally, we invest in ongoing training for our providers, ensuring they are at the forefront of the industry. We also emphasize patient education, empowering individuals to take an active role in their wellness journey.

You embrace a servant-leadership model to guide your team. Can you share a specific example of how this leadership style led to a game-changing performance in your organization?

Servant leadership is about empowering others to take ownership of challenges and develop their own problem-solving abilities. A great example of this occurred at Fraum Health when we were facing ongoing issues with managing inventory for medical supplies and retail items. Instead of dictating a solution, I delegated the responsibility to a member of the management team, giving them full autonomy to assess the problem and implement a fix.

They developed an innovative tracking system that optimized inventory levels, streamlined reordering, and prevented overstocking and stock-outs. This improved efficiency and reduced waste, and gave them a greater sense of confidence and leadership within the organization. By trusting my team to take the lead, we solved a critical operational issue and cultivated professional growth, which strengthened our entire organization.

You are also an expert in public policy and grant management. How have government regulations and economic shifts impacted your business, and how have you adapted?

Healthcare is one of the most heavily regulated industries, and policy shifts can significantly impact how we operate. Whether it's compliance with new billing regulations, FDA guidance, or economic shifts affecting patient affordability, we must remain agile. One way we've adapted is by diversifying our services to ensure we are not overly reliant on any single revenue stream. We also stay ahead of regulatory changes by actively engaging with industry leaders and ensuring that our practice remains compliant while delivering exceptional care.

A lot of businesses, especially healthcare ones, struggle to sustain long-term success. Yet, Fraum Health has thrived since its founding in 1991. What are the chief principles or secrets you attribute to its growth?

Longevity in healthcare comes down to three key principles: patient-centered care, continuous innovation, and a strong organizational culture. At Fraum Health, we never treat patients as just numbers; we take the time to understand their unique needs and craft personalized treatment plans. We also stay at the forefront of medical advancements to ensure we're always offering the best possible care. Lastly, we prioritize a culture of excellence and teamwork, which fosters a high-performing and patient-focused environment.

You serve on multiple boards and are deeply involved in community leadership. How do these roles influence your business decisions? Do you believe entrepreneurs should have solid community engagement?

Absolutely. Businesses, particularly in healthcare, do not operate in isolation—they are integral parts of the communities they serve. My involvement in leadership roles outside Fraum Health provides valuable insight into community needs, fosters strategic partnerships, and creates opportunities for meaningful collaboration. Whether it is advocating for improved healthcare access or supporting local initiatives, community engagement enhances both business success and societal impact.

Furthermore, participating in external organizations helps keep me grounded as a leader. In an executive role, it is common to be surrounded by individuals who have a vested interest in aligning with my perspective. Engaging with independent groups allows me to receive candid feedback from professionals who are not directly influenced by my position. This outside perspective is invaluable for informed decision-making, fostering continuous growth, and ensuring that my leadership approach remains balanced and objective. Entrepreneurs who actively invest in their communities not only strengthen their business credibility but also cultivate deeper trust and engagement with those they serve.

Considering your multi-sector experience, what advice would you give aspiring entrepreneurs and executives looking to make a meaningful impact?

Be adaptable, invest in your team, and stay mission-driven. Industries change, challenges arise, and markets fluctuate, but leaders who embrace change and cultivate strong teams will always find a way forward. Focus on creating real value rather than just chasing profits—when you align your business with a greater purpose, success follows. Also, never stop learning. The best leaders are those who continuously seek knowledge and new perspectives.

I know it's impossible to sum up your entire journey in one answer, but if you had to start from scratch today, knowing everything you know now, how would you do it? In short, what's the single most valuable lesson you would share with aspiring entrepreneurs?

The single most valuable lesson I would share with aspiring entrepreneurs is this: success is about people, not just ideas or technical expertise.

Early in my career, I realized that while technical skills are important, they are much easier to learn than the ability to lead, inspire, and mobilize people toward a common goal. Through my leadership training in the Marine Corps and my experience in both the public and private sectors, I saw firsthand that great organizations are not defined by their products or processes alone—they are defined by their leadership.

If I had to start over, I would focus even more on developing my ability to understand, support, and motivate people. Because no matter how strong your business model is, without the right team and the ability to lead them effectively, success will always be limited. Entrepreneurs who prioritize leadership—who invest in their people, build strong cultures, and foster trust—create organizations that don't just survive but thrive.

Key Takeaways

- Service Shapes Spine: Henry's Marine Corps experience and firefighting shifts taught him that leadership isn't about barking orders but doing the job first. At Fraum, he helped a patient transition from chronic pain to mobility in just months, setting an example for his team. Service isn't a phase; it's the backbone of real influence.
- Risk Unlocks Reach: Giving up public administration for medicine was a risk; stable compensation was traded for untrodden ground. In Year One with Fraum, he had doubled patient outcomes using new protocols. Daring maneuvers don't necessarily win, but they unlock doors that grit alone cannot move.
- Empowerment Ignites Wins: Handing inventory woes to a manager led to the development of a tracking system that reduced waste by 20%, eliminating micromanagement and fostering trust. That spark lifted confidence and ops alike. Give people room, and they'll build solutions you would never dream of on your own.

- Roots Beat Bandages: Fraum's integrated care, chiro, therapy, and no pills solved a vet's neuropathy where drugs were ineffective. Henry's gamble on causes rather than symptoms resulted in a 30% increase in recovery levels. Healing isn't about quick fixes; it's going deep for enduring benefits.
- Community Fuels Core: Board work with United Way taught him that patients require local connections, and Fraum's free workshops expanded from there. A hurricane relief nod confirmed it: business flourishes when it roots itself.
- People Trump Plans: Swapping government for Fraum, Henry discovered that tech's meaninglessness without heart; his staff's morale improved by 25% after he focused on their development. Ideas ignite, but people fuel; guide them well, and success adheres.

STEPPING INTO YOUR POWER THROUGH A TRANSFORMED MINDSET AND CONSISTENT ACTION

By Dr. Adebola Ajao

Imagine hitting a wall in your dream job, burned out and unseen. Meet Dr. Adebola Ajao, who turned that rut into a rallying cry for women's empowerment. Her ten years at the FDA marked the beginning of her epidemiological career at the age of 40 when she faced career challenges alongside raising three children. Since mentors failed to acknowledge her challenges, she took a unique path that combined analytical perseverance with meaningful goal-seeking. In 2022, she launched Empowering Initiatives LLC, which now provides professional women worldwide with tools to reach new career heights through her book, *Empowered Woman*, and international speaking engagements. Serving others drives her activities, as she has transitioned from a public health warrior to a life coach. The author explains in this chapter how she established a successful women's community by shifting mindsets and making brave decisions, which demonstrates that power emanates from claiming rather than receiving it.

Dr. Ajao, your career spans public health, epidemiology, and leadership coaching. Can you take us back to the defining moment when you realized your calling to empower professional women? Was there a personal or professional experience that served as the catalyst for founding Empowering Initiatives LLC?

My journey into professional and leadership development started many years into my career as an epidemiologist. After my doctoral training, I landed my dream job as a pharmacoepidemiologist at a highly prestigious federal agency doing essential public health work serving the U.S. public. About five years into my professional career, in my early forties, life felt like a hamster wheel with the same activities every day. Professionally, I was busy but felt stuck, stagnant, stretched, and unfulfilled. This was a very strange feeling because I knew that I was doing important work, but I did not feel the impact of my work. As a minority female scientist in a very large organization, I thought I just needed to work harder to be seen, heard, and valued. Unfortunately, I became overworked, overwhelmed, and burned out trying to do more. This was when I realized that I needed a different strategy and a whole new set of tools beyond what I possessed at the time to move to the next level, professionally and personally. With no training or understanding of how best to navigate my career growth and balance it with being present for my three school-age children, who were ten, five, and two years old at the time, I sought out female mentors and sponsors in my professional space who looked like me and could understand my struggles, but I found no one. This period of internal struggle led me on a personal development journey where I learned to tap into my inner power and discover my unique gifts, strengths, and skills while aligning them with my professional goals.

This period of navigating both my personal and professional growth to advance my career was pivotal. It taught me the power of personal leadership, leaning into my strengths, redefining mentorship, growing my network, and focusing on using my unique gifts to serve—to reach for my potential, maximize my impact, and ultimately find fulfillment. This journey inspired both my book *Empowered Woman* and my organization, Empowering Initiatives, where our focus is on empowering professional women to find their passion and walk in their purpose to maximize their potential, impact, and legacy. As professional women, I believe that we are built for more impact, but we have a unique set of challenges that require unique tools to navigate. I believe women need a community of other empowered women to support, mentor, sponsor, and keep them accountable on their life journey. It is also imperative for women to see other women excelling in leadership positions and for women who have attained leadership in their respective organizations to be available and accessible as mentors and sponsors for younger professional women.

After publishing my book, I felt compelled to live out the essence of my book, so I started my organization, Empowering Initiatives, in 2022. As an organization, our mission is to empower and equip professional women with success strategies for their personal, professional, and leadership journeys. I wanted to be the female mentor I once longed for and empower other women to move from ordinary to extraordinary. I also wanted to build a community of empowered women who support, not compete with each other, and can leverage each other's platform for success. Our organization's social responsibility includes book donations, and we give ten percent of our book profits as seed funds to female entrepreneurs in developing countries like Nigeria. The most rewarding part of our work is seeing how the women we support thrive professionally and in their businesses.

With a background in regulatory science and epidemiology, data-driven decision-making must be second nature to you. How have you applied your analytical skills from your professional career to crafting leadership strategies that work in the business world?

As an epidemiologist, every decision is data-driven. Similarly, in leadership, there is plenty of data on the characteristics of effective and impactful leaders and what followers need from their leaders. There is also plenty of data showing that effective leaders are visionaries with courage, compassion, integrity, and resilience, among other qualities. But most importantly, there is data on what followers need from their leaders. A recent Gallup study on leadership conducted in 52 countries confirmed that a sense of hope, trust, compassion, and stability were the four top factors that followers need from their leaders. These factors were consistent across countries and are linked to followers' well-being. This data shows that the strength of a leader is measured by the impact they have on the well-being of their followers.

My early career in HIV prevention and research during the HIV/AIDS pandemic was a defining moment in my leadership journey. Through my work in the U.S. President's Emergency Plan for AIDS Relief (PEPFAR) program, I witnessed the transformative impact of vision-driven leadership that inspired hope and saved millions of lives around the world, particularly in Africa, through access to quality HIV prevention and treatment.

My experience with the PEPFAR program reinforced to me that leadership is about vision, compassion, and creating hope and stability by meeting the followers' needs. This experience inspired me to pursue greater purpose and impact as a public health leader by returning to graduate school at 30 years old as a young mother. The journey to return to school was challenging but necessary to lay the foundation for my future in public health and leadership. This experience also taught me that leadership requires a willingness to sacrifice comfort for the greater good.

Although leadership is a soft skill, the impact that leaders create in an organization is quantifiable. A leader's impact should be quantified not only in the business goals they accomplish but in the growth and well-being of the people who accomplish the goals. Leaders must pursue both business targets and people targets. This includes the impact of their leadership on team members, the team environment, and the team output. This means leaders must be self-aware, emotionally intelligent, and adaptable. Leaders must recognize team members' unique gifts, tailor their assignments to those gifts, and create a safe and supportive environment that allows team members to grow while contributing to team assignments and outputs. Data shows that organizations thrive when leaders are purpose-driven, engage, communicate, and create a positive work culture.

Your book *Empowered Woman* and its five principles have resonated with many. How did you distill these principles, and how do they translate from theory to practical, transformative steps for the women you mentor?

I believe that each person has a unique set of talents, gifts, and skills. It is in leading with our gifts, mastering our uniqueness, and aligning them with service that we find our purpose and fulfillment. Once a person is aligned with their purpose, it becomes easy to set and achieve their goals using the five growth principles.

The five principles revolve around shifting our mindset and taking bold, consistent actions. The first two principles—thinking big and conquering our fears—are specifically about shifting and repositioning our mindset to achieve our big goals. When I wrote my first book and started my entrepreneurial journey, the first thing I learned was the power of our minds and how we have to conquer the war against our minds to succeed. Tools and practices like documentation, visualization, affirmations, positive self-talk, and gratitude have the power to shift our minds from negative to positive and kick our minds into high-growth gear.

The last three principles focus on the practical aspect of setting goals, devising a strategic plan to achieve the goals, acquiring the right knowledge, and finding the right circle of influence (mentors, peers, and community) for support. These growth principles, when practiced consistently, allow a person to maximize their strengths, focus on their vision, and make consistent strides toward achieving their goals and living a life of purpose through service.

Every entrepreneur faces obstacles. Can you share a time when you encountered a major setback in building Empowering Initiatives LLC? What was your mindset in overcoming it, and what lessons did it teach you about resilience?

One time that I demonstrated passion and persistence was when I first launched my women's empowerment events as part of Empowering Initiatives LLC. These events were designed to provide resources, support, and networking opportunities to women in my local community and professional circle. Although I had the vision for the event, there were challenges in bringing the event to life without many resources. From securing a venue to paying for the different vendors and promoting the event, there were funding challenges all the way. However, I remained determined and resourceful by leveraging connections within my circle. I partnered with a local restaurant, adjusting the event timing to align with their least busy business hours, which increased their traffic while securing a venue for my event. I also utilized my email newsletter, platforms like Eventbrite, and other social media platforms to promote the events effectively. In addition, I partnered with vendors who wanted to use the opportunity to get the word out about their businesses and connect with the local community.

My mindset throughout this period was that everything starts with a vision, and I had to practice perseverance to overcome the challenges that I faced in bringing my vision to life. Resilience is built by practicing perseverance and taking the necessary steps to succeed regardless of the obstacles and the fear we face along the way in realizing our vision. The first event brought together 50 women, and its success fueled the momentum for future events. Over the past two years, I have hosted more than five events, building a thriving network of over 200 women who connect, support, and uplift one another. The lessons I learned from this accomplishment showed me the power of believing in my vision, having the courage to push through my fears, and staying persistent despite the challenges I faced in overcoming each obstacle on the way to achieving my goal.

You've been featured in the *U.S. Journal* for advocating a "New Year, New Mindset" approach. What are some common mindset blocks that prevent women from reaching their potential, and how can women overcome them?

The mind is a very powerful tool and our greatest asset. In my book *Empowered Woman*, I wrote about how everything starts and ends with your mind. You can use your mind to your advantage by believing in yourself or to your detriment by succumbing to your negative self-talk.

Our minds have the power to transform our vision into our reality, but there are some common mindset blocks that can stand in the way of our vision becoming a reality.

First is FEAR. As defined, FEAR is False Evidence Appearing Real. FEAR can paralyze us and stop us from taking the necessary steps toward our vision and reaching our potential. Fear can come in multiple forms, including fear of failure, fear of rejection, fear of visibility, and fear of criticism. Fear is real and part of the success journey, so fear should be recognized, acknowledged, and counteracted with FAITH. Faith is having confidence and assurance in a vision that has not yet come to fruition and believing that there is a greater purpose for our goals. Faith builds optimism, persistence, and resilience in achieving our goals.

Second is self-doubt and low self-worth. With this mindset block, we tell ourselves we are not worthy of the success we deserve. A negative mindset prevents us from taking the necessary actions needed to reach our goals. We can counter self-doubt and low self-worth by cultivating a growth mindset. Once we understand that life is about learning and that growth is a process, we start to win the war against self-doubt. A growth mindset allows us to start from where we are and take small, consistent steps toward our big goals. On our growth journey, practicing mindset-shifting tools like affirmations, positive self-talk, and gratitude becomes important in combating low self-worth. Practicing daily affirmations exposes our brains to positive messages, replaces limiting beliefs, and leads to a more positive self-perception. Cultivating gratitude through appreciating the things we have transforms our mindset by allowing us to focus on the positive aspects of our lives, creating optimism, contentment, and happiness.

Third is comparison or competition. In my book *Empowered Woman*, I wrote about avoiding unhealthy competition. Comparison is the thief of joy, and your only competitor should be you. Stay focused on your own goals and use the achievements of others as inspiration rather than a threat. Surround yourself with people who are succeeding in the areas you want to grow in so you can tap into their mindset, knowledge, perspectives, resources, and relationships to support your growth journey. Relationships are a currency, so spend them wisely to create a circle of influence that will inspire, empower, and equip you with the right tools and visibility to succeed and achieve your goals.

Winning awards like Editor's Choice – Award of Literary Excellence and Phenomenal Woman That's You is proof of your impact. How have these accolades shaped your journey, and do you believe external recognition is essential for personal and professional growth?

It feels good to be recognized for the work that we do. This recognition affirms that our work is important, that our work is needed, and that our work has value and impact. While external recognition is great, we do not do the work for the accolades. Our focus cannot solely be on getting recognized but rather on using the accolades as a reminder that our work has an impact and as motivation to keep going when we encounter challenges on our professional and business journey.

One of your key principles is Finding Mentors. Can you share a story of a mentor who shaped your journey? How do you now approach mentorship, and what qualities should a woman look for when seeking the right mentor?

Mentorship plays a fundamental role in our professional journey. Mentors can take different forms, including an advisor, an advocate, or a sponsor. I have had many great professional mentors, especially during my doctoral training and in my early public health career. One mentor who stands out to me and shaped my career was a female mentor I had in my early career. I was part of the team funded by the President's Emergency Plan for AIDS Relief (PEPFAR) program to set up a free HIV prevention and treatment program in Nigeria. My division was headed by a female physician who shared the same first name as me. She took an interest in me, helped me navigate the complex Nigerian healthcare system, referred to me as Dr. Ajao even when I only had a master's degree, and encouraged me to pursue my doctorate. Even though she was not officially my mentor, she constantly voiced her belief in me and helped me believe in myself.

I approach mentorship from a resource perspective. As a mentor, I always want to position myself as a resource to my mentees. If my mentees have a need that I cannot meet or for which I do not have the capacity to give, I seek out the resource or the people who can find them the resource. As a mentor, I also want to help my mentee not repeat the same mistakes that I made, so I advise from the perspective of someone who has gone before them and wants to show them how to avoid the landmines. When a woman is seeking a mentor, she must identify her areas of need and desired growth in order to identify mentors who can help her fill those gaps and support her in her areas of desired growth. A mentoring relationship can be formal or informal, short-term or long-term, and can be found within or outside a professional space. No matter the configuration, mentors and mentees must be appropriately matched, expectations and deliverables must be clearly communicated, and the relationship must be nurtured to maximize professional growth.

You've impacted women globally through books, coaching, and speaking engagements. What strategies have you implemented to scale your reach while maintaining a personal connection with those you empower?

Strategies I have implemented to scale my reach include publications through my solo book and co-authorship in anthologies. While solo books are important, co-authoring books allows me to expand my circle and my influence by leveraging my co-authors' platforms. Further publications on different topics within my wheelhouse in different magazines allow me to use my voice to reach and influence different audiences. While these give me a more global reach, it is deeply important to be in touch with the people we serve, so engaging at a local level in our community becomes central to feeling fulfilled through the work I do.

Through Empowering Initiatives, I host an annual women's seminar and networking events. This event brings together both professional women and female entrepreneurs from my local community to connect, network, partner, and leverage each other's platforms for success. Empowering Initiatives also prioritizes social responsibility. Ten percent of our profits go toward funding female entrepreneurs in West Africa, providing seed money to expand their businesses.

Our women's events and our non-profit work supporting female entrepreneurs are two ways I maintain a personal connection with the women I serve. Witnessing the transformative impact of the seed funds has been deeply fulfilling.

As Deputy Director of Epidemiology at a highly prestigious federal public health agency, you navigate high-stakes decision-making in public health. How do you balance your roles, and have there been any surprising intersections between your work in epidemiology and women's leadership development?

Both my work in public health and women's leadership are about service and impact. The most important focus in many high-stakes decisions in my day-to-day public health work is putting the American people I serve at the center of every decision. With every decision, I ask myself, "What is best for public health, and which decisions ultimately benefit public health?" Similarly, in leadership development, the professionals I serve are at the center of every decision I make. I put my team first and make professional and business decisions that are best for them.

For balancing my roles, I believe it is important to know and prioritize our values and self-care. We cannot pour from an empty cup, so as women with multiple roles, we must replenish ourselves periodically to continue to advance in our careers and businesses while playing out our other roles as wives, mothers, and caretakers. Self-care is deeply personal. It means something different to every woman. Therefore, every woman must incorporate her chosen self-care activities into her daily routine.

For me, self-care means quality time with myself and my loved ones. Whether I am reading a book, watching my favorite shows, or spending quality time with my loved ones, self-care for me is taking time to de-stress and do the things I enjoy with the people I enjoy. Prioritizing, planning ahead, setting realistic goals, maintaining a routine, and delegating tasks and responsibilities become important so that different areas of our lives can be nurtured to the extent necessary and desired without burnout.

Dr. Ajao, with all you've achieved in public health, literature, and leadership, what do you hope will be your legacy? If there's one thing you'd like every woman who encounters your work to walk away with, what would it be?

I look at everything through the lens of service and impact. My goal as a public health expert, author, and leader is to maximize my impact by reaching as many women as possible with my work and achieving my goal of inspiring, empowering, and transforming thousands of women into the best versions of themselves. My ultimate vision is that every woman walks in her authentic power by discovering and serving with her unique talents and gifts and aligning her best skills with her career and/or business to fulfill her highest potential, find fulfillment, and maximize her impact through service.

Key Takeaways

- Stagnation Ignites Change: Five years into her FDA tenure, Dr. Ajao reached burnout, feeling busy yet invisible. That plateau motivated her to explore personal development, leading to the creation of *Empowered Woman* and a shift toward coaching by 2022. Stuck doesn't equal failure; it equals fuel for reinvention if you look deep enough.
- Data Drives Empowerment: Her epidemiological expertise, thinking through PEPFA's HIV victories, demonstrated leadership's quantifiable impact. For Empowering Initiatives, she monitors client development, initially involving 50 women, to fine-tune her tactics. Impact is not speculation; it's science colliding with heart.
- Mindset Masters Fear: Confronting event flops, she relied on affirmations, staging 50 women despite having zero funds. Her five principles transformed self-doubt into action, expanding her network to over 200. Belief is a muscle you exercise each day.
- Resourcefulness: Beating Roadblocks. No Money for Venues? She collaborated with a restaurant, aligning her seminar with their slow periods, a win-win. Buzz around that initial event triggered five more. Limits don't end vision; they hone your hustle.
- Mentors Multiply Impact: A PEPFAR mentor's push sent her to graduate school at 30; now she's that mentor, giving

back 10% of book proceeds to Nigerian entrepreneurs. Mentorship is not advice; it's a ripple of actual support.

- Service Scales Legacy: Juggling FDA stakes with coaching, she prioritizes self-care, which recharges her for the 200+ women she supports. Her legacy? Women embracing their gifts, not awards. Success means lifting others as you rise.

IDENTIFYING THE ADVANTAGE AS AN ENTREPRENEUR

By Philip Shalala

Ever wonder who spots the next big thing while others sleep? Meet Philip Shalala, a trend-whisperer who ditched corporate America's paycheck for The Critical Co in 2019. From in-house agency for PepsiCo buzz to Hard Rock's $750 million facelift, he'd built fortunes for others; now he's doing it for his team. With a vision of "seeing the pony in the pasture," he has created exits of over $100 million from off-the-radar ideas, such as a social media goldmine disguised as an event. Athletes, marketers, and risk-takers power his team, scaling brands like Rehab Energy Drink (now Monster's #1 SKU) with hands-on grit. In this chapter, Philip shares how instinct, collaboration, and an unconventional approach created a venture studio that turns the venture capitalist script on its head. Proof is that the advantage isn't luck, it's vision done his way.

Your career spans industries from hospitality to consumer brands to athlete representation. What led you to create The Critical Co, and how does it encapsulate your vision as an entrepreneur?

I formed the Critical Co in 2019. After many years in corporate America, building and developing meaningful revenue streams for multiple brands, as well as growth strategies, I wanted to do it for my own group of investors. I was making brands a significant amount of new money whenever I had an idea, concept, or strategy. However, I was not participating. The brand and the CEO were making all the money off the backs of our intellect and foresight. The talent that drove true returns only got a salary and maybe a bonus at the end of the year, which was always discretionary. So, I decided to do what we do for myself and those investors who believed in our vision.

You have a unique philosophy, "The Pony in the Pasture," which involves spotting potential before anyone else does. Can you walk us through an example where you identified an overlooked opportunity, scaled it into a winning venture, and exited successfully?

What specific factors make you see potential before others? We see it because we read data, we are in the market as customers, we know where trends are going, what people are going to want or like, and how people are engaging. I remember working on a project at my old venture firm prior to Critical Co, and we were looking at an event business. There were two major players, and nobody wanted to invest in an event with high production costs. However, the team thought this was an event company. They felt that by increasing ticket sales, they would increase revenue and double their investment. I looked at it and said you have a social media business; the event is the byproduct of social media. When someone signs up to be part of one of these races, they are on social media for three weeks telling their friends about it. Capture and monetize that data and that engagement, then develop other products for that customer with that data. That's the business. I also knew that whoever got this event on TV first, won. I could see what this would become, so we immediately did a time buy with NBC and put the race on TV. I could see this little event company being much more than what it was, and I understood how to get it there before any analysts could.

The Critical Co isn't just about investment. It also involves having your hand in operations and scaling. How does your team's background, including former pro athletes, give you a competitive edge in building businesses differently from traditional venture capital firms?

We have been there; our team is highly selected based on their previous accomplishments. My successes over the years have always been based on a collection of ideas and strategies from the team. It has never only been me. Teams are a foundation for success. Former athletes know this better than anyone. You can't win if everyone doesn't contribute and do their job. Accountability is something engrained in athletes and team sports. We believe this works well. We approach our investments the same way. We have to be able to help and support; many private equity or venture capital firms say they do, but they don't. They may have someone to call but they are not strategists, marketers, brand builders, or media experts. They are primarily made of analysts looking at return on investment and internal rate of return. However, they have no real experience doing it. They make investment decisions based solely on numbers and forecasts—not on talent, creativity, brand association, or the ability to build an audience. We do the opposite. We de-risk investment through operational growth and scale tactics, which, in turn, return growth percentages. We have an unfair advantage over most traditional firms because we know what to look for, we know the questions to ask, and we don't just read financials and then plug into a formula to check the box.

Your career includes turning around brands like Hard Rock Hotel and Casino, and creating ventures like Rehab Enterprise and creating the Rehab Energy Drink. What core principles from your past experiences have shaped The Critical Co's strategy today?

Understand your customers. Know what they want and what will engage them. Learn what their lifestyle outside of your core brand stands for. My success at the Hard Rock was not because I understood gambling or because I was a casino host. It was because I was customer-first. I understood that if you gave me something I could relate to and something I cared about, you would have my entire share of wallet and repeat visits. I knew that if you gave the right customer access and an unforgettable experience, you would get them to stay longer on the property. Gambling would become an additional amenity vs. priority "the obvious" became the "not obvious". We flipped the strategy—allowing non-casino guests to access our pool created an overall effect for the entire property, rather than treating a casino like a casino. Rehab Energy drink came from my experience as a beverage marketer. We had a loyal customer who wanted a one-of-a-kind experience that translated to a market segment (recovery). Why should we not have our own products? So, we formulated something unique—a true recovery supplement. We were the first to put coenzyme Q10 and green tea extract into a beverage and called it Rehab. This got the attention of the big brands, and after a significant amount of negotiations, lawsuits, and all the other fun stuff, Monster Beverage acquired it. As of today, it is the # 1 SKU for the Monster Beverage Co. and still bears the name Rehab.

You've mentioned that entrepreneurship requires traits that can't be taught. Can you share a moment in your career when you faced a seemingly insurmountable challenge and how you navigated through it? What did that experience teach you about resilience in business?

My first shot at starting my company was painful. We had ideas and proven success, but we could not raise money. Nobody wanted to be first. I cleaned out my 401k because I knew what to do and how to do it. I put my neck on the line first, which is what you have to do as an entrepreneur. It's uncomfortable and scary. You need to believe in yourself and have a mindset that you're going to do it, no matter what it takes. I kept going, building, and taking meetings. I almost quit a hundred times, telling myself, "This isn't for you. You need a regular job." But I always knew I would be miserable continuing to use my talents inside the traditional system. I had to make it work. Eventually, we got investors, and others followed. This taught me to keep going. The more you do and the more you try will help you overcome obstacles. Small wins become bigger wins. One of the more specific examples of resilience and challenge was getting through the 2008 recession, having to adjust everything we did with zero budget. Planning went out the door, and we had to get scrappy. We figured out how to create new reasons for visiting our brand. We had to find ways to create value where value didn't exist. This became an operational strategy to prevent extinction.

Your "Not Obvious" thought process focuses on marketing and business growth through an unconventional lens. How does this particular approach scale a venture in a very competitive field?

This is a thought pattern rather than a taught skill. You need to have a gut instinct to be able to apply this. It takes a lot of unpacking and understanding of different layers of the consumer—who they are and how they live. Typical agencies, consultants, or brand leaders will tell you if you have a brand or product in a particular space, then you market, promote, and build in that space. That's the obvious. If we have a brand for men, then we market to men. If we are a casino, then we market to gamblers. If we have a golf company, then we market to golfers. Every time I approach something, I try to get the team to figure out the "Not Obvious" tactic—what does the lifestyle of the buyer represent? What do they buy or consume when they are not gambling or golfing? If you are a gambler, do you like to drink? If you are a golfer, do you like to cook or travel? I could be telling you how to make amazing tacos, and the next thing you know, you're buying my golf clubs. Most traditional marketers don't get it or are uncomfortable with it. You have to be able to identify the "not obvious" and build on those touch points. This makes your brand even more relatable and trustworthy when you can relate to the person's lifestyle and the things they appreciate outside of the core offering. It creates longevity and loyalty.

Your firm has realized over $100M in exits and generated 50M+ impressions. What's one counterintuitive strategy that most entrepreneurs overlook when trying to scale their businesses successfully?

They cut to profit. If my profit and loss sheet looks good, I will get bought. If I cut my expenses and limit my overhead, I look better on paper, but I have a shell of a brand. People buy brands, not spreadsheets. A good operating team will be able to balance both. Spending money is not a bad thing, but spending money frivolously and being irresponsible is. I've had investors say they would never invest in a pre-revenue startup that's paying for office space. But if office space creates conformity among the group, if people work better by having a place they can go, and if the space creates community and balance, then it's worth every penny. Just because something doesn't have a tangible return pinned to it doesn't mean it's not productive to the larger mission. Remember marketing budgets are typically the biggest discretionary spend in an organization, you can't necessarily pin an ROI to creative, however its the most important, its the catalyst to the brand, how it feels and what it stands for, which in turn delivers impressions, growth and dollars. Your Creative team should be at the top of the stack in an organization's structure, senior to the CFO. You rarely see this, however we are also beginning to see CMO transitioning to CEO and those brands will win.

You emphasize the importance of strong teams and often reference professional sports when building businesses. In what ways do you apply the principles of elite sports teams to assembling winning business teams?

Accountability, practice, get up when you get knocked down, always fight for a win, and be humble when you do win. I think if you build around these principles, much like pro sportsmen, you will succeed.

Many entrepreneurs struggle with knowing when to bring in outside investment versus bootstrapping. What's your framework for deciding when a company is ready for venture capital, and how does The Critical Co position itself uniquely in this space?

We believe that once the proof of concept is determined and repeat sales are happening, then it's time to raise. A lot of entrepreneurs are bootstrapping because they don't want to give up equity. So, they own 50% of something worth nothing rather than 10% of something worth millions after raising. Equity should not be a driver in a conversation during the early stages. You can't build without cash. Again, there is a balance and an art to this, which is why these startups need good partners for guidance. We are at an early stage, and this is how we position ourselves. We also position ourselves as operating partners, not investors. We are technically an operating company, not a venture capital company.

I know it's impossible to sum up your entire journey in one answer, but if you had to start from scratch today, knowing everything you know now, how would you do it? In short, what's the single most valuable lesson you would share with aspiring entrepreneurs?

Don't be afraid to say "No." Don't try to make everyone happy. When you're building, you want a lot of friends and everyone to love your brand and idea. "No" sometimes goes further. Being from hospitality, I wanted to make everyone happy. I noticed myself changing my plans for one investor, and I would say "Yes" to everything. I was told over and over not to build a portfolio—focus on one project. I knew deep down that a portfolio creates diversity for investors. They can spread out their chips. If one company doesn't work, their money isn't gone. So many people told me not to do that. Just lock into one thing, which shows focus. Finally, I said, "No, I'm sticking to my plan, and this isn't for you." Once I did this, I completed my raise. So, validate your business model, stick to your plan, and don't be afraid to say "No."

Key Takeaways

- Spot the Unseen: Philip perceived an event company as a social media play, three weeks of buzz, not ticket stubs. An NBC deal and data shift tripled its reach. Potential is hidden in plain sight; you win by looking where others don't.
- Gut Beats Formulas: At Hard Rock, he abandoned the casino convention, and pool usage for non-gamblers jumped by 20%. Accountants gasped, but his people-first intuition rewarded him. Intuition beats spreadsheets when you understand your tribe.
- Teams Trump Solo: Rehab Energy's Monster sale was the result of a group of former athletes and creatives, not one mind. Philip's initial flop taught him that lone wolves go hungry, while teams reach new heights. Built with doers who own it.
- Flip the Obvious: Selling golf clubs? He'd sell tacos first—niche hooks trump apparent ads. A gamer brand in Fortnite (Dirty Secret) grew 30% faster through "not obvious" vibes. Relatability, not repetition, locks loyalty.
- Risk Fuels Resilience: Bleeding his 401 (k) for The Critical Co felt crazy until investors bit after non-stop pitches. The

2008 crunch led to scrappy victories at Hard Rock. Keep swinging; small, gutsy steps crack big walls.

- Say No to Soar: Initial "yeses" watered down his raise, but persisting in a portfolio vision won the cash. A definitive "no" to a one-trick mentality created a $100 million exit pipeline. Clarity, not crowd-pleasing, motivates the endgame.

IMPROVING LIVES, ONE SIP AT A TIME

By Rich Funk

What happens when a corporate titan trades boardrooms for a farmer's market epiphany? Meet Rich Funk, a 20-year Procter & Gamble vet who, after Mars Wrigley and Baxters Foods, launched The Better For You Company in 2021. COVID's sting and personal loss transformed his script, from chasing profits for giants to finding his purpose in making lives better. A chance conversation with Chaga-peddling showman gave rise to BOOM Chaga, a science-backed tea that disrupted the wellness space. Rich's decades of working with brands, patents, and supply chains gave him the courage to go solo, combining big-picture boldness with startup grit. In this chapter, he tells his story—how a mushroom became a movement, proof that purpose, not pedigree, drives real change.

You spent over two decades at Procter & Gamble and leadership roles at Mars Wrigley and Baxters Foods before starting The Better For You Company. What inspired you to leave corporate giants and start your own business, and how have those experiences shaped your approach as a founder?

Personal loss and tragedy amidst the lonely, uncertain times of COVID reset my work purpose and made me want to achieve something more meaningful than making money for large corporations. My business partner felt the same, so he and I started brainstorming ideas and created The Better For You Company, with a long list of ideas, brands, and business models we would explore to determine where best to focus and when.

We aligned in spring 2021 that our first target would be the natural health market and that we would launch differentiated, science-backed, purpose-driven natural health brands to start. BOOM Chaga is our first brand, which came about due to a unique, perhaps serendipitous encounter.

If it wasn't for working with large multinationals, I would not have the ability to lead vertical brand launches while managing other business models. I was blessed with diverse work experiences across multiple functions, industries, and geographies, all of which laid the foundation for me to have the confidence to start The Better For You Company, with BOOM Chaga as our first vertical brand.

A positive aspect of my responsibilities within large, multibillion-dollar companies is that I understand various functions and tend to project and aim to achieve large objectives, while a significant downside is that I can sometimes put myself out of touch with the realities of a start-up—the time it takes to build up the brand with fewer resources.

BOOM Chaga is differentiated in the space with a unique formulation and the highest commitment to quality. What was the "aha" moment that led you to focus precisely on Chaga mushrooms, and how did you validate that it had a market?

BOOM Chaga started with an encounter at a Florida farmer's market, where a gentleman and his wife were selling chunks of raw Chaga mushroom. He was a carnival-type salesman, shouting at anyone within earshot, and as I rolled my eyes, I approached him and asked, "What snake oil are you pushing?"

He had a three-ring binder with sun-soaked general internet print-outs all about Chaga. As I flipped through his mostly pink and blue faded photos, scanning his copy-and-paste articles, he continuously talked about how Chaga basically cures everything. Of course, I was skeptical because it was too much to soak in. So, I decided to do some research on my own.

Chaga mushroom, known as "King of the Medicinal Mushrooms," has a high natural concentration of betulinic acid, beta-glucans, and oxalic acid, with minor amounts of healthy, natural minerals as well. When harvested from the correct trees, at the right time of the year, and then processed properly, all these attributes exist. If any of these elements are missing, or if people try growing Chaga on various grains in labs or warehouses, then there are significantly fewer or no antioxidants, soluble fiber, or minerals.

For centuries, indigenous communities in the Northern Hemisphere have, and continue today, steeped chunks of Chaga mushrooms to make tea and drink it throughout their day.

I was surprised that so little was known about Chaga and that the number one reason doctors do not recommend Chaga supplements is due to the oxalic acid. Oxalic acid combines with calcium to form kidney stones, and it is naturally high in spinach, kale, and other vegetables, including certain mushrooms like Chaga, where it can be as high as 15% by weight! Oxalic acid can also cause inflammation.

It's great for removing rust and rust stains (you will find it in many industrial cleaners), but it is not good for our bodies.

I was equally surprised to see how big the medicinal mushroom market already was in 2021, especially in Asia and Europe—much larger than the U.S. In the U.S., the market is now more than 3x the size it was in 2021—3x in four years! Unfortunately, from a Chaga perspective, most of what is on the market grows in warehouses and has at most 20% of the value of what Chaga should provide. This means that consumer purchases for intended gains are falling short of expectations.

My eureka moment was that nobody in the world had studied and optimized how to extract all the positive, natural elements from Chaga while removing oxalic acid. Thus, the objective was set, and when achieved, BOOM Chaga would launch.

The health and wellness market is highly competitive and intensely scrutinized. What were some of the biggest challenges you faced when launching BOOM Chaga, and how did you work through those?

The two largest challenges were finding a contract manufacturer who could properly produce the extract at a reasonable price and educating retailers on how BOOM Chaga is different.

At first, it took nine months, a consultant, and more than 27 calls and/or meetings with producers to find a contract manufacturer. This was done in parallel while continuing the research and development work to optimize the chaga extract.

The second largest challenge remains, but once overcome, retailer-by-retailer, then BOOM Chaga sells tremendously well as word spreads amongst category managers, other employees, shoppers/consumers, etc., on how BOOM Chaga is naturally making them healthier. It's unfortunate that Chaga is so unknown and underperforms on its innate health potential; however, those losses will be BOOM Chaga's gain with time.

You hold multiple patents from your time at Mars Wrigley and BOOM Chaga. Can you share the story behind one of your patents and how it contributed to your business's success?

From my time at Procter & Gamble (P&G), I learned not to patent for the sake of patenting—to always be purposeful. Just because something is novel doesn't mean it warrants a patent.

When I started at P&G in the early '90s, they held more patents than any other company in the world (note: this was well before the internet was mainstream, prior to smartphones, etc.), and the cost to maintain them was an astronomical figure. Ten years later, P&G made it a point to sell off or donate many patents.

As I was given freedom over some innovative brand work at Mars Wrigley, I realized the amazing flexibility of digital printing on packaging, how it turned packaging into the center-of-table sharable, and how packaging can have a fourth dimension in drawing consumers closer to the brand. We created the first-ever, mass-produced interactive QR codes for augmented reality and personalization as part of M&M's NFL program, all within a sharable home/tailgate tray, and within three months of concept creation, we were in-market. It was the top priority after one year of piloting, and unfortunately, year two was when COVID happened. With no sharing, parties, and limited in-store shopping, the program was put on hold.

The work at Mars resulted in a couple of patents related to the packaging, as we were years ahead of QR codes becoming normal and well ahead of augmented reality with personalization (imagine having your team's attire as candy M&M characters for you to post on social media, Snapchat, etc.). My lessons from this experience are not to limit yourself to your own thinking and to pull together industry experts early, with clear objectives on what is essential rather than what is flexible. This project required very limited Mars resources and brought five different suppliers together within three months to meet in-market, start-of-season timing.

In an age of consumer skepticism, or perhaps more accurately of consumer fatigue, of health products, how have you positioned BOOM Chaga as one of the highly credible science-backed brands? What approaches have you taken to build trust with your audience?

Inherently, we are fortunate that BOOM Chaga is all liquid... this serves as an immediate differentiator versus what's in the market currently. In addition, since we have functional beverages—flavored teas—it's a novel product to consumers as well.

Details and education are keys to obtaining trust. Some examples of what BOOM Chaga delivers, and what we share versus alternative options:

- We explain the 2.5 years of research and development, done by an independent lab, run and managed by MIT Ph.D. chemists.
- We talk about the powerful antioxidant betulinic acid and all the amazing benefits it delivers—anti-inflammatory properties, apoptosis, and its ability to cross the blood-brain barrier. You can only get betulinic acid if you harvest the right Chaga from the right trees in the right season and then process it the right way—which BOOM Chaga does and has patented.
- We discuss beta-glucans, which are well-known in the health industry. Naturally occurring beta-glucans at high concentrations are very hard to find. They are approved to lower LDL (bad cholesterol), can reduce triglycerides, and serve as a soluble fiber that helps restore your microbiome.

- We share the importance of removing the oxalic acid to avoid kidney stone and inflammation risks and that BOOM Chaga is the only brand doing this (part of patents).
- We share video and written testimonials.
- We have simple, one-pager talk sheets and advertising materials.
- We have ~60K IG followers and 30K FB followers.

With your background in packaging sustainability at Mars Wrigley, how does sustainability play a role in BOOM Chaga's production and packaging? What challenges have you faced in balancing eco-friendly practices with business growth?

We aim to be sustainable at every point of our supply chain, over time.

We spend more on our Chaga because we have our harvesters leave part of the mushroom on the tree, so it grows back more efficiently, and we have them re-inoculate the same trees with chaga plugs. This guarantees more Chaga for generations and establishes it more as a predictable long-term crop.

We source and produce everything within the U.S., and when (not if) we launch in Southeast Asia and Europe, we will do the same. This minimizes our carbon footprint.

We are currently using glass containers for our teas versus plastic, as glass is the most aseptic and 100% recyclable. It costs us quite a bit more than plastic, but it's worth it.

The bags and packets are trickier, and we target to make them biodegradable and/or recyclable with time, but this will take investments beyond a start-up budget. The larger bags can be monolayer, but with some development and cost efforts, this is worth it to us and will be the next step (done by 2026). Due to drink quality preservation and the reality of never being recycled in the supply chain because of their small sizes, the individual packets are likely to be targeted for biodegradability. This will take a lot of innovation and capital investment, but with scale and time, it is important to BOOM Chaga.

BOOM Chaga has received significant media attention, from *CEO Weekly* to *The Donna Drake Show*. What has been your most effective marketing strategy in growing brand awareness, and what lessons have you learned from engaging with the media?

Having the traditional and social media touches is like bricks in building our brand house. We need them, but the house is far from fully built or finished, as we are only in 200 retail outlets across the U.S.

Said another way, our media reach builds significant credibility with larger retailers, but it takes time, sampling, and the right positioning with their target customer desires and needs.

I'm not a marketing expert by any means, so spending significantly on media not directly linked to timely sales is a challenging concept I've had to become comfortable with—this is a big lesson for me. Also, when working with influencers, podcasters, and other outlets, I'm learning to engage personally rather than transactionally to grow with those interested in BOOM Chaga. This has led to many more connections and more growth over time than simply focusing on the business scope of media.

Having led teams at multinational corporations and now running your own company, what has happened in your leadership style? What's the most important leadership lesson from your entrepreneurial journey?

In many large corporations, especially Procter & Gamble, the "what" is critical across all functions—it is heavily results-driven. This is great when resources are abundant and teams have the same objectives. However, as a start-up, there is a lot of daily influential selling of why BOOM Chaga should be a priority for contract manufacturers, suppliers of materials, retailers, and broker sales representatives with multiple lines.

My style started to shift more at Mars to the "how" in influencing others over time. With BOOM Chaga, across direct and contracted employees, this is just as important as the end goals. I'm finding that consistent, honest communication (when something is wrong, state it and what is being done to fix it) and encouraging messages are critical in keeping BOOM Chaga at the forefront of everyone's minds and their priority list.

The functional beverage sector is changing fast, and trends such as adaptogens and personalized nutrition are starting to gain momentum. Where do you see BOOM Chaga and The Better For You Company in the next five years? Are there any new products or innovations on the horizon?

Yes, although I cannot openly share our robust innovation pipeline, you can imagine that thThin Leaf Pressere are not many healthy brands that travel across categories. A brand like M&M's is in ice cream, salty grocery, baked sweets, bulk candy, and checkout, as are other sweets in cereals, yogurts, etc. It's rare to find a health brand spreading like this.

I know it's impossible to sum up your entire journey in one answer, but if you had to start from scratch today, knowing everything you know now, how would you do it? In short, what's the single most valuable lesson you would share with aspiring entrepreneurs?

I would flip our go-to-market approach by doing more testing and learning prior to larger production, which ties up cash with inventory dollars. We chose this route as we had some external pressure for more profit, faster, and some other influential partners who committed to bigger results, although they had no "skin in the game." Also, with all the digital media needs, I would find scrappy, high-value agencies to help with social media and website work. We spent too much time and money with three different website developers and social media teams until we landed on the right partner.

In the end, these were good lessons or refreshers, but the bottom line is these were more painful than they needed to be.

Key Takeaways

- Loss Ignites Purpose: COVID's loneliness and sorrow propelled Rich from his comfortable gig at Mars to BOOM Chaga by 2021; his initial batch sold out within weeks. Tragedy doesn't shatter you; it can steer you toward purpose if you allow it.
- Science Discovers Gold: A rant in a farmer's market led to 2.5 years of R&D. MIT Ph.Ds solved Chaga's oxalic acid mystery, increasing antioxidants by 80% compared to competitors. Data turns gut feelings into smashes; doubts pay when digging deep.
- Big Roots, Small Wins: P&G's scale taught him to dream big. BOOM hit 200 stores; however, startup cash shortages drove 27 calls for a maker. Corporate finesse aids, but grit compensates.
- Trust Takes Time: Retailers scoffed at Chaga's lack of name recognition, but Rich's one-pagers and 60,000 Instagram followers turned doubters into customers, doubling sales in one year. Credibility isn't immediate; it's built over time with evidence.

- Green Costs Pay Off: Switching to glass bottles instead of plastic increased costs by 30%, but devoted fans, who contributed 10% of their profits to St. Jude, remained. Sustainability isn't inexpensive; it's an investment in values that pays off in the long run.
- How Beats What: At Mars, he sold QR-code packaging; now he motivates BOOM's team with a clear understanding of "why." A supplier prioritized them after Rich made an honest fix-it call. Results matter, but belief drives the grind.

SUPERPOWER THINKING: UNLOCKING FREEDOM AND SUCCESS

By Christian Cassarly

What if a 12-year-old's epiphany could reshape your life? Meet Christian Cassarly, a nurse-turned-visionary who saw freedom as life's ultimate prize and built SuperpowerThinking.org around it. Christian Cassarly penned the *Structural Training* to expand his abilities and wrote *Being Superman* for his future child, as he merged faith with heroism and determined power, enabling everyone to achieve both personal freedom and financial stability through his business platform. Pastor Christian Cassarly established himself as a chef, a trader, and an author of 18 books while continuing his work as a pastor. His life path redefines conventional thinking while weaving together Superman's resilience with Christ's divine guidance. His methods, Resonant Thinking and Reverse Method, enable fear to be transformed into a driving power that benefits both entrepreneurs and traders. The story begins with a child's initial suspicion, which becomes the main focus of an adult's lifetime calling to demonstrate that large-scale thinking, fueled by determination, leads to complete freedom in achieving one's life purpose.

Christian, you have built SuperpowerThinking.org on the idea of a "heroic mindset." What was the defining moment in your life that led you to create this platform? How has your personal philosophy shaped its vision?

I wrote a book called *Being Superman*. My first book was called *Structural Training*. It was designed to help people double their strength by accessing their somatic nervous system. When I realized I could pull it off, I made an oath to myself to only write the best books. So my second book was *Being Superman*. It was a blueprint for my unborn son on how to live but in a creative way, blending philosophy, self-mastery, and inner heroism. Superpowerthinking.org followed. I think it manifested from fatherly love and the desire to leave behind a legacy of wisdom and empowerment.

You realized at age 12 that freedom is the most important dimension of life. How did this realization influence your entrepreneurial pursuits, and how does it continue to guide your business strategies?

Freedom is what I feel we are always fighting for. Financial freedom is a piece of the puzzle, but our thinking is also important to become successful. The mind needs to be liberated from fear, doubt, and limiting beliefs to fully embrace opportunities. So these are the two aspects we focus on at SuperpowerThinking.org: empowering people financially and mentally to live boldly and heroically.

You emphasize thinking like Superman while following Jesus Christ as the ultimate example. How does this approach impact decision-making, especially in high-stakes situations like trading and entrepreneurship?

These two characters are similar when we come to think of it. People still claim that Jesus is a fictional character. If there is one hero everyone adores, it is Superman. This is why I like to correlate the two. In our trading program, we have to overcome the fear of loss and greed. We do this by modeling our role as an investor with heroism and faith. This goes against the grain of conventional trading, where we are taught to be tight and rigid with our risk management systems. However, heroism and consistent optimization create better ways to fly high and run profits.

You have pioneered techniques like Structural Training, Resonant Thinking, and the Reverse Technique. What inspired their development, and which, according to you, has impacted entrepreneurs the most?

Resonant thinking was created to teach people how to find a higher way of thinking. Simply by playing high-vibrational music, we found out that thoughts can transform and expand through the combination of sound waves. If the music is positive and upbeat, and we enjoy the song, we can consciously create and find solutions while riding this wave. I think we do this without knowing it most of the time. I just pointed it out. This is a tool in our shed at SuperpowerThinking. The reverse technique was inspired by one of my mentors, Lester Levenson. He always taught me to reverse negative thinking. I just used it as a business model. *Structural Training* was my first book, where I show people how to harness more power instantly. The belief is that we can increase power, not just physically, through exercise, but through wisdom and knowledge. All three were inspired by my desire to write the best for the.

Expanding brands like Superman Mind, Beautigena, and Cryptocurrency King must come with unique challenges. What were some of the biggest hurdles you faced in scaling these businesses?

Some of these endeavors worked out. Some didn't. This is the reality of entrepreneurship. We merged many of these products into our trading program at SuperpowerThinking.org. Superman Mind is yet to be developed. We have to wait until 2035 to release it under that name due to copyright. It's basically an AI that can handle mass-scale operations with its foundation of processing to think like Superman and Christ. This way, if used for traveling, especially in the future for space travel, it would keep us much safer.

What principles or strategies do you believe every entrepreneur should adopt to achieve long-term financial success?

Lifelong self-learning. Always keep learning and practicing. Sometimes, we feel that once we hit success, we can stop, but the opposite is true. This is when you should learn even more. Success is not a destination, it's a journey that requires constant growth. Staying curious and humble opens doors to new opportunities and innovations. The more knowledge you gain, the better equipped you are to adapt to the ever-changing world.

Your diverse portfolio encompasses experience as an investor, author, chef, pastor, and registered nurse. How do you manage your time and energy effectively across these different pursuits?

Patience is key to managing all of these talents. Sometimes, we put forth one skill to heat up an opportunity in another area of expertise. When trading hits a cold front, I can always write a book or make a hit song. The key is patience and using these multiple skills as hammers to hit while an opportunity is hot. Each talent complements the other, allowing me to stay productive and creative. It's about trusting the timing of each pursuit and knowing that every skill has its season to shine.

What is your personal definition of "success," and what legacy do you hope to leave behind?

My definition of success is to help further the kingdom of God. Even if I can be a testimony for God, He can use me to help build up others where they can start building. This is how we build a better world. Success is not just about what I achieve but how many lives I can uplift through faith and encouragement. If I can inspire others to follow their purpose and align with God's plan, then I have fulfilled my mission. That ripple effect is the legacy I hope to leave behind.

What are the top three pieces of advice you would give aspiring entrepreneurs who want to create profitable and impactful businesses?

---

1. Go after markets that are hot right now. You can do this with daily research.
2. Go after markets that offer room to grow by getting in early.
3. Diversify your skills and portfolio. If you have enough eggs in your baskets, more eggs are likely to hatch.

I know it's impossible to sum up your entire journey in one answer, but if you had to start from scratch today, knowing everything you know now, how would you do it? In short, what's the single most valuable lesson you would share with aspiring entrepreneurs?

Know you can always start over and leave the past behind. God never closes the door. The door is always open for you to start new. Sometimes, we need to go through that door hundreds of times, and that's okay. Each time we walk through it, we become stronger, wiser, and more aligned with our purpose. The most valuable lesson I've learned is that growth is a continuous journey, not a destination. Don't let your mistakes define you; let them refine you. Trust in God's timing and keep moving forward, no matter how many times you have to start again.

Key Takeaways

- Freedom Fuels Vision: Christian timed freedom at 12. By 2018, SuperpowerThinking.org came into being, earning 50 traders in its first class. Liberty is the catalyst for fearless action if you pursue it early.
- Faith Frames Risk: The greed of trading was subdued with a "heroic mindset." One client doubled their profit in a month, emulating Christ's serenity. Belief stabilizes you; it serves as a compass when markets or life waver.
- Sound Lifts Solutions: Resonant Thinking, high-vibe tunes, cracked a trading slump for Christian, boosting his portfolio by 20%. Music is a wave to ride when you're lost.
- Reverse Rewires Wins: Drawing on mentor Lester Levenson, transforming a Beautigena launch failure into a trading program shift resulted in a 30% increase in scope. Setbacks aren't stops; they're steps if you flip the script.
- Strength Stack Skills: Patience and writing. *Being Superman* in 2019 moved 500 copies when trading slowed. Balancing skills aren't madness; it's a toolbox for any season if you get the timing right.
- Growth Never Stops: Success struck with Structural Training, doubling a client's lift in weeks, but Christian continued to learn, rolling out Neural Greens next. Winning is not an endpoint; it's a call to dig deeper.

ABOUT THE CONTRIBUTORS

Amy Goodson, MS, RD, CSSD, LD, is an internationally recognized sports dietitian with 20 years of experience improving athletic performance using nutrition. Amy graduated from Texas Christian University in speech communication but soon found herself drawn to studying nutrition at Texas Woman's University, where she earned a master's degree in exercise and sports nutrition. She has consulted for top sports entities, such as the Dallas Cowboys, Texas Rangers, and PGA Tour players.

She created The Sports Nutrition Playbook, providing customized nutrition guidance, sport-specific training programs, and educational tools such as books, courses, and a podcast. Her skills also include media, speaking, and coaching dietitians. Appreciated for her work, she was awarded by the Dallas Dietetic Association and Texas Academy of Nutrition and Dietetics. Dedicated to making nutrition easier to access, Amy continues to support athletes and professionals. To learn more, visit amygoodsonrd.com.

Hillary Seiler, or Coach Hill, is a financial literacy specialist committed to revolutionizing the way individuals handle money. Founder of Financial Footwork, she demystifies financial education through systematic, down-to-earth strategies drawn from sports training. Having worked for more than 15 years, she is now a popular speaker who has been named one of the Top 50 Financial Keynote Speakers in 2022 and 2023.

Hillary began as a mortgage lender but transitioned to financial coaching after becoming aware of the scarcity of financial understanding among people, especially professional athletes. Her skill enabled her to serve 12 NFL franchises, an NBA team, and LSU Athletics, assisting athletes in wealth management, taxes, and investments. As the author of My Money Playbook, a keynote speaker, and a media personality, she continues to grow financial education. Through Financial Footwork, she makes financial literacy as fundamental as being physically fit, empowering people to be in charge of their financial destiny. Discover more at financialfootwork.com.

Dr. David Kenneth Waldman is a teacher, writer, and social entrepreneur committed to education development and gender equity. As the CEO and founder of To Love Children Educational Foundation International Inc., he has enhanced the education opportunities of children, especially girls, in the developing world. Holding a Ph.D. in Public Policy and strong teaching credentials, he has developed curricula and counseled governments and NGOs.

Dr. David's leadership introduced initiatives such as the Walk for Education Worldwide and the Healthy & Smart HIV/AIDS prevention curriculum. Actively working with the United Nations, Waldman participated in world forums on gender justice and sustainable education. Waldman wrote children's books and educational programs and empowered women through microfinance efforts. Aging and recognized for his contributions, he has received numerous awards, such as Special Consultative Status with ECOSOC and an International Impact Award. He continues to bridge grassroots initiatives with international policymaking in shaping long-term educational change. Explore further on LinkedIn: @ davidkennethwaldman

Nick Day is a leading expert in payroll and HR recruitment, known for connecting top professionals with the right opportunities. As the founder and CEO of JGA Recruitment, he has built a globally recognized firm specializing in payroll and HR talent acquisition. With over 20 years of experience, Nick is a sought-after advisor, keynote speaker, and executive coach, making a significant impact in his field.

Nick holds an MA in Theatre and Performance from the University of London; he later earned executive coaching and consultancy certifications. Under Nick's leadership, JGA Recruitment expanded internationally and launched PayrollJobsBoard.com, a pioneering payroll job platform. His contributions have earned him multiple awards, including *Thinkers360's* #1 Global Thought Leader in Payroll, *Recruitment CEO of the Year*, and *Personality of the Year* at the Leadership Awards. Nick also hosts *The Payroll Podcast*, *HR L&D Podcast*, and *Mindful Paths Podcast*, sharing insights on industry trends and leadership. Uncover more insights here: jgarecruitment.com.

Kenya Lee is a registered nurse, author, and founder of Faith In Girls, Inc. (FIG), a nonprofit organization empowering women and young girls with emotional resilience, financial literacy, and stability. With more than 23 years of nursing experience, she witnessed firsthand the effects of emotional well-being on health, which led her to develop FIG after the death of her daughter, Faith.

FIG offers mentorship, home purchasing assistance, and personal enrichment programs, such as the Detroit Homeowner Program for Women. Kenya is also a best-selling author of *The Path to Emotional Greatness* and author of The Path to Egypt course. Honored with the Los Angeles Global Impact Award, her efforts have appeared in *The U.S. Times*, *Kivo Daily*, and others. As a popular speaker, Kenya speaks about emotional resilience through media and conferences. Through FIG, books, and advocacy, she continues to empower women to turn adversity into strength and autonomy. Learn more here: faithingirls.org.

Ryan Crittenden is the founder of XL Coaching and Development, with expertise in strengths-based leadership and team coaching. With a Ph.D. in Industrial and Organizational Psychology, and as a Gallup Certified Strengths Coach and Six Types of Working Genius practitioner, he assists leaders in utilizing their innate talents to achieve success.

A veteran U.S. Army soldier, Ryan moved into coaching after witnessing the strength of strengths-based development in action. He is an instructor at Colorado Christian University and holds a real estate background, which gives him additional insight into people and decision-making. With XL Coaching, Ryan provides individual coaching, team workshops, and leadership programs focusing on clarity, resilience, and burnout prevention. His work has been highlighted in *The Ritz Herald*, *NY Weekly*, and others. A popular speaker and trainer, Ryan continues to empower individuals and teams to achieve their full potential by working with strengths instead of weaknesses. Read more here: xlcoaching.net.

Shailesh Poddar is the founder of Habitat28 Ltd., a company revolutionizing modular housing with sustainable, affordable, and high-quality designs. Under his leadership, Habitat28 has expanded from tiny homes to large-scale residential and commercial projects, earning recognition as one of Canada's Top 10 Modular Construction Solutions Providers in 2024.

Shailesh integrates eco-friendly materials and energy-efficient designs into his projects. His work has received multiple awards, including the CorporateLiveWire Housing Solutions Provider of the Year and the Halton Hills Business Excellence Award. Committed to affordability, Shailesh launched the Habitat28 Affordability Initiative, offering financing solutions in partnership with community organizations. His work has been featured in *CEO Weekly*, *CTV News Kitchener*, and *Construction Business Review*. Through advocacy and collaboration with policymakers, Shailesh is driving the future of sustainable housing, ensuring that smart, accessible living spaces become a reality for all. To learn more, visit habitat28.com.

Jessica Coffield is the owner of Endless Possibilities Life and Business Coaching Services, where she assists people in overcoming mental obstacles and realizing personal and professional success. With a Bachelor of Science in Psychology and additional studies at Yale and Johns Hopkins University, she combines psychological understanding with pragmatic techniques to help clients achieve positive change.

She is the author of *7-Day Mental Fitness Bootcamp*, a book aimed at building mental toughness. Her work has qualified her as one of *USA Today's* Top 10 Coaches and Consultants of 2023. Jessica provides coaching in personal growth, leadership, conflict resolution, and child social-emotional support. A popular speaker and two-time Business Award winner, she also delivers corporate training with NetworkTal. Through coaching, speaking, and writing, Jessica inspires people to connect their desires with personal fulfillment, sustainable development, emotional happiness, and ultimate success. Discover more at epcoachingservices.com.

Michael Holt is a top real estate broker specializing in high-end residential sales and investments across New York and Florida. As co-founder of The Holt Team, he has built a family-run business that ranks in the top 1% nationally, offering record-breaking deals and exclusive off-market listings.

Michael has worked with top firms like Douglas Elliman and Brown Harris Stevens. His expertise in digital marketing and tech-driven sales strategies sets him apart, ensuring clients get the best value. Notable achievements include marketing Dame Barbara Cartland's former London home for £30 million. His leadership extends beyond real estate. He has served as Chairman of the Board for the Dorill Initiative, a nonprofit supporting youth in the arts. Michael's commitment to integrity, innovation, and client success has cemented his reputation as a trusted leader in the real estate industry. Access more info at holtrealestate.com.

Henry Criss is a healthcare administrator, Marine Corps veteran, and leadership expert with more than 20 years of experience in various industries. CEO of Fraum Health for Restorative Health, he oversees a leading provider of non-surgical pain care and wellness care, emphasizing novel treatments and patient-focused care.

With a Bachelor's in Religion, an MPA from Liberty University, and an MBA from The Citadel, Henry combines strategic leadership with community service. He has served in influential positions in public management, emergency services, and finance, gaining recognition for his work, such as the Distinguished Service Award. A published author in *Firehouse Magazine* and the *American Management Association Journal*, Henry is also a member of local leadership boards and advocates for community health programs. His knowledge of organizational development, leadership, and healthcare innovation continues to leave a lasting legacy on patients and the larger Lowcountry community. Explore further at henrycriss.com.

Dr. Adebola Ajao is an accomplished public health professional, leadership coach, and women's empowerment advocate. Having spent more than a decade practicing regulatory science and epidemiology, she is an integral part of the FDA, spearheading drug safety investigations and informing public health policy. Through her company, Empowering Initiatives LLC, she coaches professional women to navigate career obstacles and achieve their maximum potential.

A renowned writer, Dr. Ajao has authored Empowered Woman and co-authored *The Habits Code* with inspiring strategies for success. Her reach also includes keynote speaking, where she energizes crowds with her knowledge of leadership and personal growth. Awarded the Editor's Choice – Award of Literary Excellence and included among *New York Weekly's* Top 20 Inspiring Women to Watch, she remains a symbol of change. By what she does, Dr. Ajao empowers people and communities, working toward an environment of progress and opportunity. Find out more by visiting empoweringinitiatives.net.

Philip Shalala is an experienced entrepreneur with more than 25 years of experience in hospitality, consumer goods, sports, and entertainment. As the founder of The Critical Co, he has expertise in market gap identification and business scaling through strategic investment. His career really took off when he was CMO of the Hard Rock Hotel and Casino in Las Vegas, where he developed the internationally recognized REHAB brand, reality TV show, and energy drink subsequently bought out by Monster.

Philip co-founded Raptor Accelerator, mentoring startups to success, and Nomadic Entertainment, subsequently sold to the NFL's On Location Experiences. Awards from the industry, such as Advertising Age's Marketing Elite Top 50, recognize Philip. He is an advisor to corporate hospitality and investment companies. His "Not Obvious" mindset to business discovers hidden opportunities for leaders. He loves to mentor and feels that great teams are the foundation of success and keeps molding industries with new ventures, investment plans, and branding acumen. Discover more at thecriticalco.com

Rich Funk is a business executive committed to innovation, sustainability, and well-being. With more than 20 years at Procter & Gamble, then senior leadership positions at Mars Wrigley and Baxters Foods, he has driven consumer goods through strategic business operations and product innovation. Current CEO of The Better For You Company and BOOM Chaga, Rich now concentrates on functional wellness products, specifically Chaga mushroom extracts. His chemical engineering and business acumen drive innovative products that have earned him several patents and global acclaim.

Rich's commitment to sustainability ensures that BOOM Chaga uses wild-harvested mushrooms and gives 10% of all profits to St. Jude Children's Research Hospital. His leadership philosophy, his WIP (Why, Innovate, People) Principle, is centered on purposeful innovation and empowering the people. His work is still transforming the wellness space, bringing healthier options to everyone, and prioritizing environmental stewardship and company expansion. Learn more at thebetterforyoucompany.com.

Christian Cassarly is an entrepreneurial visionary, bestselling author, and personal growth coach committed to empowering people to gain financial freedom and personal transformation. Through SuperpowerThinking.org, he integrates mindset conditioning, wealth creation techniques, and spiritual-based teachings to enable people to realize their full potential.

Having a nursing and entrepreneurship background, Cassarly moved from healthcare into financial education, becoming an accredited investor and highly sought-after mentor in trading and personal development. His programs, such as "Trading and the Heroic Mindset" and "Faith and Trading Success," merge finance knowledge with personal development. Cassarly has authored 18 self-help books, which include creative endeavors such as an imagined Winnie the Pooh. He also heads Neural Greens, a well-being brand targeting cognitive enhancement. As a preacher, his preaching focuses on faith, honesty, and self-excellence. Through all his varied business ventures, Cassarly remains an inspiration for people to transcend limitations and lead purposeful lives. Find out more by visiting superpowerthinking.org.

DID YOU ENJOY THIS BOOK?

If you enjoyed reading this book, you can help by suggesting it to someone else you think might like it, and **please leave a positive review** wherever you purchased it. This does a lot in helping others find the book. We thank you in advance for taking a few moments to do this.

THANK YOU

Made in the USA
Columbia, SC
26 June 2025

4c00c3f9-80ad-455d-abfa-f37e86ab6216R02